FAMILY TIES

Relationships, Socialization, and Home Schooling

Gary Wyatt

University Press of America,® Inc.

Lanham · Boulder · New York · Toronto · Plymouth, UK

Copyright © 2008 by
University Press of America,® Inc.
4501 Forbes Boulevard
Suite 200
Lanham, Maryland 20706
UPA Acquisitions Department (301) 459-3366

Estover Road
Plymouth PL6 7PY
United Kingdom

Library of Congress Control Number: 2007936082
ISBN-13: 978-0-7618-3911-8 (paperback : alk. paper)
ISBN-10: 0-7618-3911-9 (paperback : alk. paper)

To Ranae

Contents

Preface

The research reported here relies on a 12-year participant observation study of home schooling from the perspective of an author who is a sociologist and the father of both home and traditionally schooled children. Long-term participant observation studies afford the opportunity to provide a depth of meaning to an area of inquiry that questionnaire research cannot provide. Consistent with most studies of this kind, I make no effort to use quantifiable techniques that produce statistical findings. Rather the qualitative nature of this research provides the description and explanation of observations and insights gained during this period of time.

Despite growing acceptance, home schooling remains controversial and, as a home schooling parent, I cannot ignore the controversies or pretend that nothing personal is at stake. What I can do is be fair in my observations of home schooling's strengths and weaknesses. Much of the literature on home schooling is polemical in nature as home schooling proponents launch attacks on the failings of public schools and present home schooling as a near utopian alternative. They tolerate no criticism of home schooling and immediately become defensive as critics raise concerns about the practice. Critics counter that home schooled children have re-stricted social lives and do not receive an education equal to that provided by traditional schools. They argue that home schooling is a retreat from the social contract and represents a harmful fragmentation of society.

While my purpose is to provide insights into home schooling from the perspective of its practitioners, I will not present an idealized image of the practice. Home schooling worked very well for some of my subjects, not at all for others, and somewhere in between for the rest. Like any other human activity, home schooling has its strengths and weaknesses. Neither should be ignored.

Three themes emerged central to the home schooling experience: First, the desire for, and the importance of, strong family relationships and for creating families that are, from a sociological point-of-view, true primary groups. Second, concerns about the social world children experience at traditional schools and about current cultural ideas about childhood and parenting. Finally, the desire of home schooling parents for heightened amounts of autonomy and independence in their personal lives and in the lives of their children.

During this time period, I had the opportunity to interact with and observe countless home schooling families. I am indebted to them for their friendship and for sharing their lives with me.

Gary Wyatt

Emporia, Kansas, May 2007

1
School's Out

Society provides us with warm, reasonably comfortable caves, in which
we can huddle with our fellows, beating on the drums that drown out the
howling hyenas of the surrounding darkness. "Ecstasy" is the act of
stepping outside the caves, alone to face the night (Berger 1963, 150).

Many books have been written on home schooling. My first task is to make
clear the purpose of this book. Most books written on home schooling focus on a
list of familiar topics related to the history of the home school movement (Lines
1991; Knowles, Marlow and Muchmore 1992; Stevens 2001), its ideological and
pedagogical schisms (Van Galen 1991), academic efficacy (Ray 1997; Ray and
Wartes 1991), rationale for and defenses of home schooling (Guterson 1992; Holt
1982) and strategies for would-be practitioners (Colfax and Colfax 1988). These
topics will receive minimal attention here.

The purpose of this study is to explore some less obvious but powerful motives
for, and outcomes of, home schooling. The motives and outcomes I will focus on
relate to the type of relationships home schooling parents want to have with their
children, with concerns they have about the social world children experience at
school and with certain aspects of the conventional wisdom about parenting, childhood and adolescence. Socialization, the process by which people learn the ways
of their culture and develop a concept of self, will be central to this discussion.

William I. and Dorothy S. Thomas (1928, 571-72) wisely observed: "If
[people] define a situation as real, it's real in its consequences." Sociologists have
long noted the importance of the "definition of the situation" for the behaviors
people engage in and the personal identities they assume. Thus, the process by
which home schooling families come to define formal education as undesirable, opt
for home schooling and take on the identity associated with it will receive
considerable attention here.

By directing my focus to relationships as prime motives, I do not mean to imply that home schooling parents aren't concerned about academics and religion, two issues frequently associated with home schooling. Nor am I calling into question the research of scholars who have explored the home school movement and found that these issues are indeed major motives for home schooling (Mayberry et al. 1995; Ray 2004). Much of this research, however, relies on survey research methodologies and, like any methodology, survey research has its strengths and its limitations. One of its limitations is that it cannot provide the "depth of meaning" that participant observation can provide. Many of my findings are not the kind of findings that subjects would provide as they complete questionnaires. These findings emerged slowly over time through conversation, observation and reflection. Consequently, my work compliments rather than contradicts previous research findings. Academic, religious and pedagogical issues are important but they are not the only motives for home schooling. While familial relationships have been identified in the literature on home schooling (Mayberry et al. 1995, 92-93.), they have not been explored in the detail that I will attempt to do here.

I appreciate the words of the renowned sociologist Peter Berger (1963, 23) who has written: *[T]he first wisdom of sociology is this: things are not what they seem.* Berger reminds us there are official reasons for existing social realities and then there are less obvious and sometimes obscured reasons for those same realities, reasons that can be more powerful than the official ones. This insight is relevant here.

I will show that the official motive for home schooling, namely providing children with a quality educational and often religious experience is no more important than the less obvious, often unarticulated motives of home schooling which are: 1) developing, maintaining and enjoying relationships and patterns of interaction with children that are substantively different from what they would be if those children were formally schooled and 2) providing a means of resisting elements of both the dominate culture and the youth subculture that many home school families find objectionable. Some of these objections relate not only to what these parents consider the current state of affairs to be in public schools, but also often arise out of their personal experiences with public schools when they were students themselves. These past experiences relating to social cruelty and academic frustration are an important catalyst for the decision of many of my subjects to home school their own children. I found that these motives apply to many home schooling families regardless of their political, spiritual and pedagogical differences.

The findings presented in this book resulted from a number of sources: First, my own experiences for the past twelve years as a home schooling parent and those of my wife, Ranae, and our three sons. We removed our two oldest sons from public school during the conclusion of their 5th and 3rd grade, respectively. They were home schooled all the way through high school. Our oldest son just graduated college and is preparing for graduate school. Our second son is fluent in Spanish and has taken a hiatus from college while he performs service work in south central Phoenix. He will return to college shortly. After seven years of home schooling, our third son requested enrollment first as a part-time public schooled student and now as a full-time public high school student. He is having a good experience there. Home schooling worked very well for our two oldest sons and public schooling is working well for our youngest.

My second source of information includes interaction between and relationships with numerous home school parents and children from several Midwestern states over a twelve-year period. This interaction involved friendships with individual home schooling families, participation with several home school support groups, correspondence from young adults home schooled as children, attendances at home school conventions, campouts, lobbying efforts and other social events, and interaction online in a number of venues with a large number of home schooling parents and children from across the United States. Finally, I also make use of the published writings of home schooling participants in a variety of periodicals and books. The identities of all subjects will be protected. All names embedded in the quotations provided by all subjects are pseudonyms.

All of the parents in my study were educated in traditional schools, either public or private, and their children are the first generation to be home schooled. This is important because a second generation of home schooling families is beginning to emerge, that is parents who were home schooled as children are now just beginning to home school their own children. The motives of second-generation parents will likely be different from first-generation parents, many who had negative experiences with traditional schools. I can say little about second-generation home schoolers, and studying them is the topic for another study.

My exploration of home schooling is informed by symbolic interaction, a sociological perspective that focuses on making sense of the social world by analyzing the interaction that occurs between individuals at the interpersonal level and the meanings that emerge out of this interaction (Colomy 2005; O'Brien 2006). A tenant of symbolic interaction is that to understand the human experience, it must be done from the subjective point of view of the people experiencing it. Sociologist Herbert Blumer (1969, 56) has written:

> Symbolic interactionism requires that the inquirer actively enter the worlds of people being studied in order to "see the situation as it is seen by the actor, observing what the actor takes into account, observing how he interprets what is taken into account."

A goal of this book is to enable the non-home schooling public to understand home schooling from the perspective of these participants themselves. In the pages that follow, I will, therefore, attempt to give home school participants voice as they describe their motives for home schooling and their experiences with it. I will provide my own insights as well. Regardless of the judgments readers may make of the views expressed in the pages that follow, those views are real for the people who hold them and are the basis for action. Understanding, not agreement, is my goal.

The main research strategy used here involved participant observation, a method that focuses on observing human subjects in natural settings as the researcher interacts with them as an active participant. As a home schooling parent who regularly attended a variety of activities, conventions, meetings, and the like, my work as a researcher was secondary to my motive to be a good home schooling parent. Nevertheless, my participation in these activities provided me with ample opportunities to interact with and observe a broad spectrum of families.

The results I report will be "descriptive" rather than "statistical" in nature. This "qualitative" methodology does not generally employ questionnaires or sampling with the statistical analyses typical of such studies. I must emphasize that I will not generalize my results to all home schooling families nor do I claim to be a spokesperson for the home school movement. While I believe my results are characteristic of many home schooling families, I will limit them to the subjects in my study. In order for statistical analysis of home schooling to be representative, a questionnaire must be administered to a random sample of respondents drawn from a list of all home schooling families and an adequate response rate of returned questionnaires must be achieved. No sampling frame listing all home schooling families currently exists nor do I believe one ever will. Sampling of home schooling families in previous research has generally been limited to those associated with specific groups. Even then, the low return rates these studies have achieved are problematic. Thus, while I cannot generalize my findings to the population of all home schooling families, other more "statistical" studies suffer from comparable limitations.

As a sociologist and practicing home schooling parent, the issue of "objectivity" must be addressed. In the academic world there are at least two approaches to this problem. The "positivistic" approach is based on an "objective" researcher who selects topics, observes what he or she is studying, and then reports the findings in a value-free and unbiased way. The "postpositive" approach rejects objectivity as impossible, potentially deceptive, and, in many cases, undesirable (Schroll 1988). This approach claims that there is an inescapable relationship between the observer and the observed and because of this relationship a researcher is not capable of being truly value-free or unbiased. While the goal to be as objective as possible is attempted, it is acknowledged that despite researchers' best efforts, their perspective and life's experiences will influence the interpretation they place on what they observe. The call here is for one of awareness and honesty. Researchers must acknowledge their perspectives so that readers are aware of their points of view from which researchers see the world.

As a subscriber to this perspective, I have determined to be up-front about my views and, by so doing, inform my readers of my perspective. While I will make every effort to be objective, I, like anyone else, perceive the world through the lens of my personal perspective and life events. I offer the following statement: *I am a sociologist with a background in the study of family, education, and socialization, and a parent who has found home schooling to be successful and rewarding. It worked best for some but not all of my children. I do not believe that home schooling works for everyone nor do I offer home schooling as an educational panacea. A variety of educational alternatives are needed in contemporary society including public, private, charter and home schools.*

The insights I offer here emerged gradually and unexpectedly as I interacted with my subjects and as I examined my own experience and evolving motives. This "process of discovery" raises an issue I must address. As my own motives evolved, did I impose my "definition of the situation" on my subjects and read into their motives that which I, not they, were experiencing? I've thought about this a lot as I've examined not only my data but my interpretation of it and I do not believe this is the case. While there is an inseparable relationship between the observer and the observed, I believe that I genuinely experienced separately that which I observed in others. I believe the process of developing our "careers" as home schooling families nudged us to experience similar realities. The relevance of Berger's insight offered above occurred to me after the fact. I originally approached this study believing that home schooling was predominantly about educational quality and in some cases about religious issues. It wasn't until the other motives emerged in conversation and observation time and again that I realized home schooling was a relationship issue as much if not more than an educational or religious one.

Before proceeding, a definition of homeschool is in order. Home schooling is difficult to define because home schools differ from each other as well as from the majority of contemporary educators and students. The word *home school* is misleading in that it suggests a definition based on location-the place where the learning supposedly occurs. It also suggests that parents are teachers, the children are learners, and the home is the center of the educational experience. Years of experience with home schooling has shown me that this is often not the case. Home school families, I have found, are providers and recipients of an education who rely on a wide array of resources to meet their academic goals. Home schooling, therefore, is neither a place nor exclusively a family program, but an educational experience that is planned and implemented by parents and children. Home schoolers are not necessarily what the word home school implies, namely those who receive an education at home. *Rather, home schooling is an umbrella term that applies to a variety of ways of obtaining an education with the help of one's family, outside of formal institutions.*

Currently, the home school movement is deeply divided over a variety of pedagogical, philosophical and political issues. Some seek to define themselves and their ilk as true home schoolers while dismissing others as non-home schoolers. These divisions take place on issues such as religion, structured and unstructured approaches to learning, and on the use of resources provided by public and private schools including online courses and prepackaged curricula. My definition of homeschooling includes all of those listed above. I did not exclude any subjects based on any of these issues.

Home schooling can be viewed as a process of sorts, that is to say a social phenomenon with ongoing issues that need to be addressed. For the subjects in my study, four dynamic issues occurred and reoccurred. These issues were 1) discontent and concern with traditional schooling, 2) commitment to home schooling, 3) managing identities, and 4) adjustment and adaptation. Although these issues are to some extent sequential, they are often experienced simultaneously. I refer to them as dynamic because they ebb and flow. They influence and are influenced by each other. They are resolved and then resurface to be resolved again as conditions change.

For the first-generation home schooling families in my study, the decision to home school was influenced by concerns with traditional schools and the life styles that resulted from involvement in them. Commitment to home schooling was influenced not only by the perceptions of the traditional school experience as unsatisfactory, but by the perception of home schooling as an intrinsically rewarding experience. My subjects would sometimes evaluate and re-evaluate the quality of the traditional school experience based on their evaluation of their home school experience. If home schooling didn't work, then traditional schooling would be re-evaluated and placed in a more positive light and vice versa.

Identities are negotiated ideas of who a person is. They are negotiated between that person and the significant and generalized others in his or her life. Is that person wise or foolish, worthy or unworthy, respected or disrespected, legitimate or illegitimate and so on. Members of the home school movement work to negotiate favorable identities with the non-home schooling community in an effort to achieve a sense of legitimacy and acceptance. Finally, adjustment and adaptation involve the personal lifestyle consequences of home schooling and the changes that are necessary to make it work. Socialization, relationship issues and academic success are all issues here.

The book will proceed as follows: Chapter 2, *Another Brick in the Wall*, will explore some reoccurring characteristics of families in my study and the experiences that pushed them away from traditional schools and the lifestyles embedded in it. Chapter 3, *The Road Less Traveled*, will focus on the forces that drew them to home schooling and motivate them to either continue in the practice or to abandon it. I will show that disliking traditional schools is often motive enough to begin home schooling but not enough to sustain the practice. No matter what the reason-academic, social, religious or otherwise-home schooling will not be successful if relationships between parents and children don't emerge that make it a positive and rewarding experience.

Chapter 4, *The S Word*, will provide an in-depth look at socialization and home schooling. As home schooling parents know, issues related to socialization, referred to by many as the "S Word," constitute ground zero for the controversy swirling around this practice, and it is in this area that most criticism of home schooling is levied. This chapter will delve into the process of socialization and its consequences for both home schooled and formally schooled students and families. It will examine cultural issues surrounding parenting, gender roles and family life that prompt both the criticism of home schooling, and, for many families, provide a major motivation for it.

Chapter 5, *Doubles and Fears*, focuses on the anxiety that home schooling families experience and the strategies they use to manage it. The importance of reflected appraisals, impression management and identity negotiation strategies characteristic of most human interaction are applied to home schooling. Home school families and organizations have, with considerable success, tapped into societal concerns about public education and the youth subculture to legitimize home schooling. Some segments of the home school population, however, launch vitriolic attacks on public schooling and trumpet home schooled students' academic accomplishments to further legitimize this practice. I will suggest these strategies are double-edged swords and, if the home school movement is not careful, their arguments can backfire and lead to charges of isolationism, fanaticism, and elitism. Furthermore, the image presented by some home school organizations of home schooled children as geniuses can present not only daunting expectations for families who aspire to but cannot achieve such unrealistic and exaggerated outcomes, but also lead to attacks by skeptics about sampling bias and generalization problems inherent in the interpretation of some of studies advocates cite to justify home schooling. A more cooperative and less confrontational approach to educational and cultural issues is needed now that home schooling has, to some extent, become more acceptable (Knowles, Marlow and Muchmore 1992).

Chapter 6, *Challenging Assumptions*, summarizes the role of home schooling in contemporary society, most notably its role as an alternative lifestyle, a reaction to what has been labeled the permeable postmodern family (Elkind 1998). I will argue that home schooling is not an effort to "turn back the clock" to a mythical 1950s style "golden age" of the family, but rather it is an effort to establish the family as a true primary group regardless of what the past may or may not have been.

2
Another Brick in the Wall

There is a time to admire the grace and persuasive power of an idea,
and there is a time to fear its hold over us. The time to worry is when
the idea is so widely shared that we no longer even notice it, when it
is so deeply rooted that it feels to us like plain common sense. At the
point when objections are not answered anymore because they are no
longer even raised, we are not in control: we do not have the idea; it
has us (Kohn 1993, 3).

The first home schooling family I met was decidedly unimpressive. I had never heard of home schooling before I met this family and I was surprised and dismayed by them. Their motive for home schooling stemmed from the mother's belief that the school system in our conservative, republican, church-going community had somehow been overrun by "communists" and "secular humanists" bent on corrupting her children. Her pronouncement of belief was, of course, greeted with bewilderment and consternation by educators at the neighborhood public school, most of whom were conservative, republican, church-going types themselves, and were surprised to learn of their true identities as minions of Beelzebub. Needless to say, her kids spent their days hanging out in their backyard, swinging on a tire swing, and riding their bikes around town. When asked to read a passage in church or in some other situation, the kids proved to be functionally illiterate. Home school, I concluded, was another name for truancy.

While this family's motive for home schooling is typical of some of the families I encountered in my exploration of home schooling, it is not typical of all or even most. Home schooling cannot be reduced to a single ideology or motive. The same can be said for the outcomes this family experienced. While I dismiss as methodologically flawed some of the studies that have been made public over the past years, that I will discuss later, touting home schooling as a producer of geniuses on a mass scale, most of the home schooling children I have encountered appear to have received a respectable academic education.

Why home school? Human motivation is very complex and is often influenced by a variety of variables which may include past experience, values, beliefs, societal constraints and opportunities, and even biological and genetic variables. After interacting with home schooling parents for many years, I have concluded that the decision to educate one's own children is very complex as well. As I explored with individual parents their reasons for home schooling, a list emerged, and while some of those reasons endured for the duration of the home school experience, others faded away and new ones took their place. The reasons families begin home schooling are not necessarily the reasons they persist.

Some readers who are vaguely familiar with home schooling might take exception with my position. They believe, as many have told me, that home schooling is about religious extremism and that families like the one mentioned above are the rule not the exception. This view is too simplistic. While religious motivations figure prominently into the decision of many, they do not figure into the decision of all; and even the devout have other motivations as well. I have encountered precious few home schoolers, religious or otherwise, who are extremists by any definition. While deviant types are unlikely to wind up as subjects in sociological studies like mine, I remain certain that despite their penchant for alternative forms of education, most home schooling parents are responsible and respectable in far more ways then they are not. They hold jobs, have mortgages, pay taxes, and are integrated in their communities as volunteers, neighbors and citizens. Their children watch TV, hang out at the mall, eat fast food, take piano and karate lessons, join boy and girl scouts, and attend church youth groups. While these children may not be as involved in the youth subculture as their same-aged peers, they are in many ways normal kids. As home schooling continues to become more acceptable and commonplace, I believe the validity of these observations will become more pronounced.

Home schooling is after all not a creation of the religious right, it emerged out of the anti-establishment counter-culture of the 1960s and 70s. The social ferment from whence it sprang was probably more libertarian than conservative. Social conservatives joined the movement after that and, currently people from a variety of persuasions are involved in home schooling in increasing numbers. Home schoolers are currently a politically, socially, spiritually and pedagogically diverse lot, stereotypes to the contrary.

General Observations

Before proceeding, I will offer some observations of the home schooling families that inform this study. First, for the majority of them, the decision to practice home schooling was made by women who often needed to convince somewhat reluctant husbands and children of its benefits. I have not encountered a single family where husbands pressured wives into home schooling against their

will although I'm sure there are those who have. The following comments are typical of the people I've encountered:

A mother:

> When I first brought the subject up to my husband, bless his heart-I don't
> think he really knew what he was getting into-I brought it up more as a suggestion
> and then proceeded to provide him with more and more and more reasons why it
> was necessary. It wasn't too hard to convince him, he wants what is best for our
> children just as much as I do, and it is also obvious to him that ps [public
> schooling] does not necessarily equate with education.

A father:

> After a visit with my son's teacher I finally gave in and agreed with Kari that
> we should home school our children. She believed she could best teach them the
> Christian point-of-view that way but I hesitated for quite a while. When our son
> continued to have problems and his teacher couldn't do anything about it, I finally
> gave in.

A largely unarticulated motive for home schooling emerged in conversations
with many of these women. Most were women of substance who made the personal
decision to be stay-at-home-moms when they could have chosen otherwise. The
decision to establish home schools presented them with the opportunity to transform
homemaking into a role that more fully tapped into their abilities and creativity.
Planning and implementing learning activities of various kinds required them to
read, think, experiment, communicate, problem solve and network. Home schooling
presented them with an alternative version of home making that stimulated and
engaged them more than routine home- making alone might have done.

Second, in the vast majority of home schools I've known, mothers are the
primary teacher/facilitator. While husbands provide varying levels of support,
women are the heart and soul of home schooling. Thus, while I will often refer to
the behaviors and opinions of home schooling parents in this book, it should be
understood that I am primarily talking about women, most of whom I would
estimate to be in their late 20's or 30's during the time the research for this book
took place.

Third, most home schooling families are by definition single paycheck
families. While most families that I have encountered possess the financial
resources to exist on a single paycheck, the majority do so at considerable economic
sacrifice. Nevertheless, they seem willing to forgo the materialism of two incomes
in order to pursue what they consider to be a more meaningful lifestyle. Home
schooling is to at least some extent a rejection of materialism. While I have met few
families who are paupers, their material standard of living is generally diminished.
The words of one home schooling mother, while a bit extreme, illustrate this
diminishment while acknowledging that their condition results from a choice they
have freely made.

> Now I do not work and we have very little in the area of material things. Our computer is even a dinosaur... We rent our home, we drive a 12 year old car and at times have walked and taken the bus, we buy second hand, we grow our own veggies, we don't "go out" but opt for "family time" at home, there are a ton of things working people have that are only a dream for us. But our sacrifices are worth it in our eyes.

While not as economically strapped as the family above, a young mother with two young children offers her reasons for the decision she and her husband have made.

> For me having children was a choice. It was something that happened because my husband and I desperately wanted it to happen. I didn't have children so that the state could take them away from me when they turned five or six and keep them for most of their waking hours until they turn eighteen. I gladly quit my career to raise my kids. I want to be the one who teaches them to read, to add and subtract, and who opens their eyes to the wonders of the world. I don't want the life that forces me to get up early, scramble to get myself and the kids dressed, get them to school and me to the office, come home late and tired only to repeat the same exhausting routine day after day. I know it means doing without the things we could buy, but I have chosen a different life and I wouldn't trade it for the world.

Fourth, home schooling involves an enormous amount of time and effort on the part of home schooling parents. Although there is variation here with parents who favor the structured "school-at-home" experience spending time teaching, developing lesson plans, preparing activities, and grading assignments, and parents favoring a less structured "unschooling" experience engaging in learning-related activities and in providing an educationally rich environment, time and effort are major expenditures for all home schooling families. The time and effort spent home schooling is time and effort that can't be directed on other activities.

Fifth, there is a substantial outcomes risk involved in this decision. Because parents in general, and mothers in particular, have invested so much of themselves in home schooling, and because they are by choice the major agents of education and socialization in their children's lives, they have a lot at stake. If the children struggle academically, socially and personally in life, these parents are more likely to shoulder the responsibility and bear the guilt for those troubles. They can't blame the schools or peer groups as other parents can. This is a reality of which home schooling parents are keenly aware.

Sixth, there is relationship risk involved in home schooling. Home schooling families are with each other much of the day. With this level of closeness, the possibility of developing deep and meaningful relationships is very real, so, too, is the potential for conflict. Interpersonal issues emerge that cannot be ignored because there is nowhere to hide. If the home school isn't working, it can become very stressful for all. While home is indeed a haven for most of the families I have encountered, it is not for all of them. In my experience, home schools that fail do so for relationship reasons more than academic ones.

I hasten to add that traditional schooling comes with considerable relationship risks as well. With the separation and isolation it exacts from families, relationships between parents and children can deteriorate. In her longitudinal study of the social lives of adolescents, Hersch (1998) describes teens in her long-term study as occupying a social world apart from and invisible to their parents. I will explore this issue in more detail in the socialization chapter.

Seventh, some families take a surgical approach to home schooling electing to home school one or two of their children while sending the others to traditional schools. When asked about this arrangement, they would reply that home schooling was what one child needed for this reason or that but not what their other children needed. This mainly occurred if one child was really struggling at school while the others seem to be doing reasonably well. A few families began home schooling with the goal of doing so for only a few years and then enroll their children in traditional schools at some pre-determined point in time. Elementary, middle and high school transitions provided natural breaks for these enrollments to occur.

Eighth, although home schooling has earned a marginal amount of acceptance, there is still considerable societal disapproval of it. In some cases, these parents are labeled religious fanatics, overprotective, controlling, anti-social, elitists, isolationists, and even child abusers by others. Some members of the general public that I have spoken with express concern and suspicion of home schooling. They worry that children will be social misfits who lack the academic knowledge and social skills to function effectively in society. Consequently, home schooling parents can be subjected to criticism, ridicule, and rejection. This is particularly true if the children do not appear to be doing well academically or socially. This heightens the pressure on these families to produce successful children and to negotiate favorable identities.

Finally, while the majority of the parents I got to know were active participants in a variety of religious faiths, they were either the only members of their congregations who home schooled their children or one of a few who did. While they seemed to receive some support at church for their decision, there is little evidence that they selected home schooling to comply with dictums received at church. While there may well be congregations filled with home schoolers, I didn't encounter any in my study.

I will now provide insights offered by parents about their decision to home school their children. The following are representative of comments that I heard time and again as I interacted with parents over the years. These comments center on the experiences they had as students in traditional schools years earlier and, in some cases, with experiences their children had in school before they decided to withdraw them.

Parental Academic Experiences

Some of parents I encountered indicated that their academic experiences in school were less than ideal. The comments range from concerns expressed by those who were good students by conventional standards to those who struggled academically. A notable sentiment repeats itself in these reflections, one of school as a place unfriendly to a student's natural curiosity, where compliance is the major expectation.

One mother stated:

> I accepted school. I did well academically, athletically and excelled socially. I suppose I could be the social child everyone thinks about with the socialization question. I only had to give up creativity and clarity for this wonderful privilege of conforming. I had loads of friends, excellent grades and not one thought of my own. It's humbling to admit, but if a teacher or authority person didn't tell me how to do something I could not do it, yet by their standards, I was an excellent student.

Another mother offered:

> I did well in school . . . I quickly learned how to jump through "their" hoops and do things "their" way to get approval yet I learned next to nothing in school and hated most of it. . .I did well had a high IQ and read on a college level by grade 3. I don't want my children going through this and wasting 30 years of their life like I did. I want them to be thinkers, and dreamers, and doers' not conform-ists, and machines, and robots.

Finally, a father who disliked the entire school experience described his feelings this way:

> It was the anti-intelligence attitude. I hated the teachers who could turn the most fascinating material into sawdust. . . I hated the dumbed down material we were stuck with. I hated the fact that anyone who showed a modicum of intelligence was treated with contempt and was ridiculed. Not one single teacher in the high school was inspiring, in fact they came close to crippling my interest in every kind of literature with the exception of science-fiction (since they didn't allow us to read it, they couldn't ruin it for me).

The images these comments conjure, that of school as a lock-step place, has received considerable support in the research on schooling. Jackson (1968) des-cribes what he has labeled the "hidden curriculum" of schools and compares it to the "official curriculum." Jackson states (pp. 33-4),"[T]he crowds, the praise, and the power that combine to give a distinctive flavor to classroom life collectively form a hidden curriculum." While the objective of the official curriculum is to master academic material, the objective of the hidden curriculum is that of conformity and obedience. In a classic study of kindergarten, Gracey (2001) ob-served children as their school experience unfolded. While school officials promoted the learning and creativity that kindergarten offered, Gracey found that the major function of kindergarten was to teach children the "student role" and the key component of that role was compliance, namely learning to do what they were told to do, when they were told to do it, whether it makes any intuitive sense to them or not. While some might claim that learning to do what one is told is a necessary and important lesson of life, that lesson is certainly not the official version for the existence of school.

Kozol (1992) and Gatto (1992), two former teachers, have written that compliance is a major lesson taught in schools, particularly for low-income students, most of whom will later as adults accept service sector employment where "doing what they are told" will be the major job requirement. As a result of years of classroom experience, Holt (1964) argued that typical classroom activities induce fear in children that they deal with by employing a series of defensive strategies that by their very nature stymie learning. A father in my study reflects his views of the consequences of formal schooling.

> I believe that spending most of the day indoors with two dozen kids the same age is unnatural, unhealthy, and very, very limiting. Children need to see much more of the world than that. Schools promote the status quo, conformity, obedience to authority, passivity, intellectual dependence, emotional dependence, group identity, intergroup conflict, hostility towards achievement, and antipathy towards thought. Oh, yeah, and they are a colossal waste of time.

Parental Social Experiences

Considerable research has been about the social world at traditional schools. A review of this literature will be presented later when socialization is discussed in Chapter 4. Until then, I will briefly outline generally-accepted points relevant to school-based social life. First, with the advent of mass schooling, children and adolescents were placed in public and private schools where they spent their days in relative confinement with others their age and largely removed from the adult world. Second, as a result of this segregation, a youth subculture emerged. A component of this subculture is a stratified social system in which popularity, status, inclusion and exclusion are major dynamics. Consequently, many youth find themselves in an intense social environment where peer influences and social cruelty are the norm. Finally, the social world at school differs noticeably from the social world they will experience later as adults. While adults are subjected to inclusion and exclusion, the intensity is diminished as adults are not confined at close quarters to an age-segregated world, and they tend at least on the surface to behave differently than children and adolescents do when interacting with others.

The social realities of formal schooling generally overwhelm the academic ones for many students. For many years, I have asked students at the university were I work to describe what was most memorable to them about their K-12 experience. What they share are social experiences such as football games, proms, friends, love interests, acceptance or rejection. Academics are rarely mentioned in these discussions, and when they are, students generally reduce this conversation to the grades they earned or to a particular teacher they liked. No one has mentioned a moment when they "connected with Shakespeare" or when "the quadratic equation suddenly made sense."

As a result of the triumph of social forces at school, those who do not fit in can be in for a difficult experience, one that haunts them for years to come. I am impressed and saddened that years later, many otherwise competent, well-adjusted and successful parents in my study weep over the troubles they experienced years ago at school.

Interviews with parents suggest that these experiences influenced their decisions of some of them to home school their own children. Consider the written comments of three mothers below:

Mother 1:

> I absolutely hated the social aspect of school. I was always despised because I did well academically. The name "the brain" with a certain tone and snarl comes to mind. And definitely I wasn't in with the "pretty" crowd. It took me many years to get over the damage to my self-esteem that no high GPA could overcome. You couldn't pay me enough money to go back to junior high or high school but I am not so sure that it was the fault of the school or just the teenage thing.

Mother 2:

> I had few friends, inconsistent grades and plenty of thoughts of my own. I probably liked kindergarten, but I hated school for the twelve years after that. I got in all sorts of trouble for not fitting in, and I was that "lucky" child who was always teased. Oh, yes, I was extremely bored as well, and since I'm not the kind who cleverly manipulates the system (I just straightforwardly fought it) I wasn't able to get to do interesting work on my own instead of the boring, elementary stuff the class was doing. To put if simply, the entire thing was a horrible experience and I wouldn't wish it on my worst enemy.

Mother 3:

> I hated school! I wonder how many home schoolers hated it. I spent most of the school day daydreaming, and basically learning things on my own time at my own pace, and that interested me. I never felt like I fitted in with my age group. The girls seemed to always be forming "clubs" worrying about who was dating who . . . I am still very upset about what experiences I had in grammar school. . . . I finally had enough and in the middle of my senior year "dropped out" got a GED and started college. My son is now 4 months and we're planning on having another child. Neither will ever set foot in a traditional school.

A father reflects back on his experiences and offers the following:

> My family did not tease me in any way, but in school it was merciless. I was always the youngest and largest and clumsiest. Small kids would harass me knowing that if I retaliated physically I would be seen as the big bad guy. I was terrible in sports and too fascinated in things for my own good. My family tried

to provide a refuge, but I was in school six hours a day! How could I find refuge? As much as the system of schooling has driven my intellectual decision to homeschool, it was the abuse I received at the hands of my peers that has driven the decision emotionally.

The emotion in these comments is palpable and the conclusion is clear: These parents are motivated based on their childhood experiences. School to them was a hurtful place where bad things happened. Home schooling is a defensive strategy initiated to ensure that their children are not subjected to the torment that defined their childhoods.

Children's Social Experiences

Another common motivation that continually emerged in conversations with parents was the negative experiences that their young children had at school before home schooling began. Most of these involved social cruelty such as hazing or bullying. The reason I believe issues related to social cruelty were such significant motives centered on their visibility. Attentive parents can easily detect the tell-tale signs of a tormented child. Furthermore, physical and emotional danger prompt immediate action as protecting children is one of the highest duties of parenthood. Few things will motivate parents to action more than a victimized child and most parents will do whatever it takes to protect them. Consider the comments from two parents below.

Mother 1:

My son attended public school for k-4 grades. I sent him off to school a sweet little boy eager to learn all he could, excited about going to school, loving books and finding out new things. He was outgoing, friendly, rarely down, very confident. What I got back was a child scared of a number of "bullies", com-pletely down on himself (he asked for a knife to kill himself because he couldn't handle the pressure), zero self esteem, convinced he was a failure, withdrawn and a loner... Now that he's been home two years he is out of his shell, loves to read, loves learning and seeks out new information on his studies all on his own.

Mother 2:

I mentioned that Michael has had a bit of a problem with teasing from other children I guess that every child has a bit of that and it's just part of growing up. We have been very concerned with the amount that Michael has had to put up with. It's a lot different than when we were in school. I can't imagine being called the names he has been called or having the profanity that is hurled at him. He is a very bright child and is ridiculed for it. For a long time we brushed it off and just considered it part of growing up. Brian and I have talked long and hard about the situation. We came to the conclusion that neither of us, in any of our dealings with adults, have ever had to face what Michael faces every day at school. I think that one of the things that has frightened me the most is the fact that he is beginning to accept it as normal treatment of him by his peers. If an adult was put into that situation they would be very quick to call it abuse and do something about it. Since it is as the school level then it is just "part of growing up".

The treatment of special needs children at school served as a significant motive. Although not as common a motive as social cruelty, challenges that confronted both gifted and learning-disabled students were frequently cited. Parents of gifted children worried that their children were not being challenged and that school presented a social experience that devalued academics in favor of athletics, popularity and the like. Parents of learning-disabled students were often vocal and highly motivated to intervene.

> A big benefit of homeschooling was, frankly, for me. I knew my heart would break if yet another teacher complained to me daily about Walt's behavior. It took so much effort to try to be charming, to try to get teachers to consider alternative ways of dealing with children, to face their frustration and anger with Walt. I too, couldn't figure out how he could be such a monster at school, when he was always fine when I observed, and when he was very reasonable at home. I don't doubt that he really was a monster at school—and although I do blame the schools for much of his behavior, he still did act poorly, and schools will not tolerate that well.

The frequency of these types of experiences and their entrenched nature in traditional classrooms has been recorded by observers. In his cross-national studies of classroom behavior, Olweus (1993) has documented that absent adult intervention, bullying occurs in virtually all classroom settings. Holt (1981, 44-45) offers the following description of the typical school:

> If there were no other reason for wanting to keep kids out of school, the social life would be reason enough. In all but a very few of the schools I have taught in, visited, or know anything about, the social life of the children is mean-spirited, competitive, exclusive, status-seeking. snobbish, full of talk about who went to whose birthday party and who got what Christmas presents and who got how many Valentine cards and who is talking to so-and-so and who is not.

Children's Academic Experiences

Negative academic experiences of children were also mentioned, although not as often as social experiences. The comments in this area centered on the fear that a child was struggling and that the school seemed unable to intervene. The following comment from a parent who eventually removedthis child from school is typical of this genre.

> We've been concerned about Dale's learning level at school. He's an OK student but we are concerned about how much he is actually learning. He's not the fastest learner in the class and when you are just one in a large crowd it's easy to get lost in the shuffle. We've talked with his teacher about our concern and she too is worried. His work is rushed, sloppy and often incorrect with many missed problems. She says she'd like to do more but cannot give him the attention he

needs because she has other student to teach. Each year he seems to fall a bit more behind.

Because social life dominates the school experiences of students, social motivations top the reasons parents in my study were initially motivated to home school their children. Academic reasons were significant as well. As I have stated earlier, I believe relationship development between parents and children are major motives for home schooling, although I have said little of that in this chapter. That motive emerged later as the home schooling career of my subjects unfolded, and it proved to be a major factor sustaining and rewarding the practice.

Motivation Concluded

In sum, while some parents who look back on their own school days with warm memories may select home schooling because they have come to believe that the quality of traditional schooling has deteriorated since they were students, many of the home schooling parents I know give their own school experiences less than flattering evaluations.

I am aware of the argument that social conservatives and the media have created a "manufactured crises" whereby a never-ending drum beat of negativism directed towards public education has produced a widely-held, yet inaccurate, perception of incompetence and ineffectiveness (Berliner and Biddle 1995). This argument holds that parents are opting for private schools and home schooling because they have been duped into believing that public schools are failing when in fact they are not. The motive for manufacturing this crisis is ultimately to divert public funds from public schools thus weakening a perceived "government strangle hold" on education.

I agree that socially created definitions of the situation can be powerful motives regardless of their veracity, and perhaps public schools are not failing to the extent that people believe they are. Undoubtedly, there are parents who had positive school experiences as children but have come to believe either correctly or incorrectly that contemporary schools are inadequate and that private schools or home schooling offer a necessary anecdote. While I will not dispute that possibility, I suggest that claims of incompetence will resonate more convincingly with those who had bad experiences at school. My argument is that if far more students past and present had positive experiences both academically and socially with traditional schooling, the motive for and frequency of home schooling would diminish considerably. So long as a substantial proportion of people, both parents and children, had (or have) negative experiences, home schooling will remain a fixture on the educational landscape regardless of whether contemporary schools are or are not in crises. Consider the words of a young mother who offered this conclusion.

> The decision to home-school was a pretty easy one. You all know how it is when you have that first baby during those late night feeding sessions and you think about everything. While contemplating education, it didn't take much

reflecting about my own [public school] experiences to realize that there was no way I was going to send my children to public school.

3
The Road Less Traveled

Emily: Do any human beings ever realize life while they live it?—every,
every minute? Stage Manager: No. The saints and poets, maybe—they do
some. (Wilder 1938, 124-5)

The decision to begin home schooling was often a difficult one. The will to
continue was no small task either. While some acclimated to home schooling with
relative ease, others had considerable difficulties with many adjustments to make
and much explaining to do. Some immediately found home schooling to be a
positive experience and embraced it, some found it fraught with difficulties and
abandoned it, others found a mixture of both good and bad which they weighed in
the balance and proceeded accordingly year-by-year, sometimes day-by-day. The
transition to home school is a substantial undertaking. Not everyone was able to
make the adjustment.

The decision to begin home schooling occurred when parents came to define
their concerns with traditional schooling as serious enough to require consideration
of an alternative like home schooling. In addition to concerns about educational
quality and cultural, relationship issues were motives for home schooling. While
relationships were seldom the motive prompting parents to home school in the first
place, for many families I know, they emerged as a serendipity of sorts, an
unexpected and yet satisfying outcome that sustained them in the practice.
Emotionally satisfying relationships provided a motive to continue in what would
otherwise be an exhausting undertaking. The following written response from a
home schooling mother who describes teaching her little girl to read illustrates both
the importance of learning and the emotional rewards of home schooling.

> We have a large chalkboard and while I held my arms around Jamie she
> wrote the letters and we sounded the words out together. What a joy for me to

hold my daughter in a hug while she learns to read. And how stress-free for her
to learn against Mom while she discovers this puzzle called reading! As we sat
there on the floor with the chalkboard in front of us I thought, "This is why I'm
home-schooling. She's safe, secure and enjoying learning."

Another parent articulates two frequently expressed sentiments: the first,
getting to know her children, and second, the desire to be with them.

> I got to know my sons really well. In addition to loving them I found that I
> liked them and liked being with them. While some of my friends say they are
> overjoyed when school starts I didn't feel that way. I missed my boys when they
> were in public school. While we certainly have our days when things didn't go so
> well, my oldest son particularly can be quite strong-willed, but they were the
> exception more than the rule. For most days the good over-weighed the bad and
> I found my self enjoying having them near.

I believe this desire to be with children is in part a reaction to a culture that
increasingly separates parents from children. The rise of adult organized and
supervised after-school activities that reduce the unstructured free time children
have to pursue their own interests or spend time with their families has been
analyzed by social sociologists (Adler and Adler 1994). This "extracurricular
career" occupies children's time while their parents work and prepares children for
the corporate world that they will enter as adults. Some parents I know define
quality parenting as the practice of enrolling children in as many organized
activities (i.e. soccer, karate, scouts, band, lessons of various kinds, etc.) as
possible. These children have day planners and handheld computers to keep track
of their schedules. Their days involve being rushed from one adult- organized
activity to the next, and most of their waking hours are spent under adult
supervision. Elkind (1995) comments on these recent social changes and their impact on family dynamics by comparing what he labels the contemporary "permeable
family" with the "modern family" of an earlier time.

> In keeping with the new sentiments of the permeable family, a new value has
> emerged that reflects the direction of these sentiments. This new value is *auto-
> nomy*, whereby each family member pursues his or her own interests and puts
> these interests before those of the family. In the modern family, where together-
> ness reigned, having meals together took precedence over individual pursuits.
> Today, soccer practice, music lessons and business meetings take precedence over
> sharing mealtimes. If the nuclear home was a haven, the permeable home is more
> like a busy railway station with people coming in for rest and sustenance before
> moving out on another track. (p. 13)

Social tendencies often provoke backlashes as segments of the population
come to resist them. Home schooling is a tool in this resistance. The parents cited
below found home schooling to be an anecdote to this new type of family.

A mother said, "I enjoy being with my children, especially when we are at our
best, not tired, not stressed. I love to learn with them."

Another added:

> I have a grin on my face a mile wide as I watch my kindergartner outside with his
> older brother working on "bicycle mechanics." Of course, now that their bikes are in
> tip-top working order, they need to be cleaned off. The patio is soaked and so are the
> boys and I'm sure that most of it came from each other. Today we've read, including
> my 5-year-old, done some math, talked about the museum that we went to on Friday
> and its relevance to the Civil War, cooked, written stories, played on the computer,
> rolled 700 newspapers for their 1 day a week paper route, worked on a science project,
> talked about some camping ideas and worked on some Boy Scout goals. We all know
> everyone's names, nobody got pushed down outside and we're all happy and feeling
> pretty productive.

The majority of the home schooling parents I know would say that despite the
difficulties and stressors involved in home schooling, the good days outnumbered
the bad, and they developed satisfying relationships with their children because of
it. Home schoolers who persisted were generally successful home schoolers, and
much of that success depended on how emotionally and socially rewarding they
found it to be. Their views can be compared with those of university students I have
interviewed over the years about their high school experiences. As university
students reflect back on their high school days, they recount friendships, football
games, proms, and teachers they liked. They say little about issues of academics
and learning. The social realities of high school overwhelmed the academic ones.
University students either loved or despised high school based on emotional rather
than academic experiences. The same holds true for home schooling.

Home schooling parents who struggle often abandon the practice. Their
reasons centered on relationship problems, role conflict, and stress.

> Daniel wouldn't do anything I asked. Minor disobedience problems erupted
> into big ones. He would mouth off to me and every assignment turned into a
> never-ending series of power plays. After a year of turmoil and nothing getting
> done, I ending it.

Daniel responded with the following: "This really sucked. No friends to hang
out with and being around my mom all day was the worst. Probably the worst year
of my life."

Another set of parents described their family's failed attempt at home
schooling.

> We tried home schooling Kenton because he was having lots of trouble at
> school, flunking classes and getting in with the wrong crowd. It didn't work at all.
> He was so terribly disrespectful to his mother. It was a damaging experience for
> her. I don't know if their relationship will ever be good again. I'd come home and
> she'd be crying because of the things he'd done. He'd do things to deliberately get
> under her skin. . . It really got to me. He's the schools problem now. At least Heidi
> has some peace while he's there. I don't mean to vent, but this didn't work.

His wife concurred with his views and added the following:

> There were far more bad days than good ones. I felt so stressed all the time.
> I just couldn't get him to mind me and I got so tired of trying to do it all. It was
> just too much. I wondered at times if we [son] even liked each other. It was better
> before when he was off to school and I didn't have to deal with him and his antics
> every minute. Home schooling was stupid idea anyway.

The degree of stress and role conflict weighed into the decision of one
overwhelmed single mother to call it quits.

> Here I go. I'm finally admitting it. I can't do it all. I can't be mother, teacher,
> dishwasher, cook, and work part-time. I have no time to my self. Sometimes I
> think I'm going crazy. So this ends it. Tomorrow I am going to check out schools
> in my area and if I can afford a private school he's going there. If not it's back to
> public school. It just didn't work and quite frankly I'm worse for the wear.

Finally, a woman who recently moved nearby indicated that she was going to
enroll her once home schooled children in the local public school. Her husband had
never been supportive and this had caused a few problems. She also mentioned the
effort involved in home schooling a large family and the positive feelings she had
about the quality of schools in her new community.

> [T]he teachers were much better. They taught the way I wanted my child-
> ren to be taught so I said why not. I feel a bit like a sell out but I think I'm doing
> the right thing. Maybe I can help them more at home by not being both teacher
> and parent.

Home schooling, like many things human, is about relationships. Relationships
and the interaction that takes place in them form and shape our identities, our world
views, and in many ways our well-being. The quality of our relationships influences
the quality of our lives. Home schooling made that point clear and, at its best,
presented an opportunity for parents and children to forge deep and meaningful
relationships and, at its worse, tore them down. Home schooling was a catalyst that
strengthened good relationships and further eroded weak ones.

4
The "S" Word

Everyone's childhood is normal to them (Anderson 2007, 59).

Two home schooling mothers were at a local park with their children. It was a beautiful September afternoon. The sky was clear blue and the leaves on the trees were turning yellow and gold. There was a hint of autumn in the air, just right for outdoor play. Suddenly, a woman approached the mothers and asked why their children where not in school. The mothers explained that their children were home schooled and were at the park for some physical exercise. The inquiring women regarded them coldly. After a while, some other children on their way home from a nearby elementary school joined the home schooled children at play. After a few minutes, however, it was time for the home schoolers to go. As their mothers attempted to retrieve them, they found their way suddenly blocked by the woman, who now made no effort to conceal her contempt. "At least let these kids have *some* fun with other children their age!" she fumed.

At a general university faculty meeting a number of years ago, an old acquaintance approached me and began a conversation. The subject of family came up and he asked how my children were doing in school. I explained that my kids were home schooled and that they didn't attend public school. He had heard of home schooling and had serious reservations about it.

"Who will protect home schooled children from fanatical parents who may force their dangerous political and religious views on them?" he worried. He had heard that members of extreme right-wing anti-government groups home schooled their kids. Many home schooling parents, he suspected, were like those parents.

"Don't get me wrong," a concerned teacher said to me, "I know home schooled kids are smart but what about their socialization? Those that I've met are solid academically but they are so withdrawn and quiet. It's like they're afraid of their own shadows. They can't talk to anybody. They don't fit in."

A home schooling parent was chided by her sister, "Sooner or later," her sister said, "you've got to stop being so protective. Your kids must be allowed to experience the real world. Think of what they're missing by not being in school: no recess, no school plays, no band, no football team. They'll even miss the prom. How can you deny them these important life experiences? Home schooling is not good for either you or them. C'mon, cut the apron strings. Give your children the freedom and independence they need to grow!"

The authors of a college textbook (Thompson and Hickey 1996, 229) argue that home schooled children encounter "restricted social interaction" and "do not experience the diversity that can be provided in the social arena of the schools." They suspect that home schooled children "may be ill equipped to function successfully in the larger Multicultural world."

All of these concerns have something in common. They focus on socialization. "What about socialization?" is the question that beleaguers home schoolers more than any other. One mother said, "My parents believe we are going to turn our son into a social moron because we home school him . . . I think when I die the question 'What about socialization' will follow me into the grave." Queries posed to parents about socialization are far more common than those involving academic concerns. They center on the quality of interpersonal interaction, social relationships and opportunities, or lack thereof, that critics suppose home schooled children have. "What about socialization?" is also a question loaded with assumptions about what's best for children, families, and society. While concerns about socialization are the most pointed and common criticisms the home school movement receives, concerns about the socialization are some of the most common reasons parents give for home schooling in the first place. Many parents have told me that if there were no other reason for home schooling, the peer-based socialization that occurs at school would be reason enough.

My experiences and observations as both a researcher and a father of both home and public schooled children lead me to the conclusion that both sets of parents should be concerned about socialization. I've known many home schooling families whose children have rich and satisfying social lives as well as some who are limited, cloistered and deprived. I've also known many traditionally schooled students whose experiences at school have been uplifting and positive, and many whose experiences have led to social, emotional, legal and academic problems. Generalizing about either experience must be done with caution.

I will begin with an exploration of what socialization is and will proceed with an exploration of the research on life at school and the kind of socialization children and teens experience there. I will then review research findings on the socialization home schooled students experience and will conclude this chapter by adding some of my own insights and observations.

What is Socialization?

Socialization has been defined in many ways with most definitions focusing on social interaction as the cause of a variety of outcomes including the integration of the individual into society, the learning of cultural norms and values, and the formation of the human personality (Tallman, Marotz-Baden, and Pindas 1983, 21-27). Most definitions compare socialization with learning and education. Brookover (1964) wrote:

> Actually, therefore, in the broadest sense education is synonymous with socialization. It includes any social behavior that assists in the induction of the child into membership in the society or any behavior by which the society perpetuates itself through the next generation. (p. 4)

I define socialization as the process that occurs through interaction in which people learn the ways of their culture, are integrated into society, and negotiate identities. Implicit in this definition is that notion that through socialization three things happen: first, a culture is reproduced; second, individuals assume their respective places in society; and third, their identities are negotiated.

A culture is defined as the beliefs, values, expected behaviors, language, and material objects that people in a society share. A society is a large collection of people who live in the same geographical area, are generally subjected to the same political and economic order, and enact a common culture. An identity is a negotiated definition held by a person and the people he or she interacts with on a regular basis as to who that person is (Gecas 1982, 10). I include negotiating an identity as opposed to focusing on personality formation because I am convinced that components of the human personality result in part from genetic and biological factors (Gallagher 1994) while an identity results from interpersonal interaction and is socially constructed.

Virtually all human beings experience the socialization process (Elkin and Handel 1989, 8-25). The exceptions include but are not limited to people with severe biological problems that render interaction and learning impossible, children raised in isolation, and adults in long-term solitary confinement of one kind or the other. Consequently, the criticism that home schooled children are not socialized is moot. Rather, their socialization experiences are different from traditionally schooled children.

Referring to her childhood experiences as a home schooled student and to the criticism about her life being restrictive and "unreal," Swann (1989) wrote:

> People frequently ask me, "But what will you do when you get into the real world?" I am then tempted to ask, "What makes you think that my world is any less real then yours?" After all, reality is relative. The world of a teenage runaway is certainly not real to Nelson Rockefeller's daughter, any more than the world of an Ethiopian who grows up, lives and dies in a famine ridden country is real to the average, middle-class American. Who is to say which of these worlds is "real," since each is so different from the others? . . . The life I enjoy may not be typical but it is most certainly real, and I can think of no better lifestyle. (p. 76)

Swann's point is correct. People with the aid of others around them create their own realities based on their personal experiences and social situations.

Not only do people experience different environments but they experience the same environment in different ways. During the course of this study, I have interacted with a large number of traditionally schooled young people who've participated in several youth organizations where I have served as an adult leader and counselor. Two students who are alike in many ways and attend the same neighborhood public school do not have a common experience. Characteristics like athletic ability, physical appearance, social skills, social class, gender and race have substantial impacts on the experiences children have at school, even if it's the same school. The founders of American public education envisioned public school as a "common school," a place where children from diverse backgrounds would have a common experience. That vision has never been realized.

The same is true of the home schooled children I know. The personal traits and characteristics that children possessed combined with the quality of the relationships they had with their families produced diverse experiences for all involved. For many children, home schooling was a positive experience, while for others it was more problematic.

Because socialization involves learning the ways of a culture or subculture, I will briefly review characteristics of the contemporary youth subculture that children experience at school (Bynum and Thompson 1989, 251-67). The youth subculture is widely considered to be a creation of industrialization and mass formal schooling where young people were removed from meaningful adult roles and placed in schools where they spent their days in relative confinement with others exactly their age (Gottlieb, Reeves and TenHouten 1966). Left to themselves, young people created their own subculture which included but is not limited to the following characteristics: 1) status hierarchies of groups and individuals; 2) peer dependence; 3) distinctive styles and fads; 4) unique slang; 5) marginalization and powerlessness, and 6) values and norms that are often in opposition to those of their parents (Eckert 1989; Hersch 1998; Milner 2004; Sebald 1968, 206).

Market forces including the electronic media have recognized the youth subculture and marketed products such as music, movies, clothing, jewelry, cosmetics and other material objects to teens. By so doing, they reinforced the boundaries separating them from their parents and other adults. Home schooled children are more influenced by the environments created in their homes by their parents, their siblings and themselves, and by those in the outside world that they interact with on a regular basis. A difference then between home schools and traditional schools is that children in home schools are influenced more by parents and siblings, and traditionally schooled students are influenced more by peers and the youth subculture described above (Delahookie 1986). I exclude teachers because research shows that traditionally schooled students spend only about one percent of their time interacting with them one on one (Schneider, Csikszentimihalyi, Knauth 1995, 183-84).

Life at School

Most school children live lives so routine that we fail to give them the scrutiny they deserve. A fish, Percy (1985, 178) once observed, does not think about water. "He cannot imagine its absence, so he cannot consider its presence." Like Percy's fish, schooling is so ubiquitous that there is much about it that we fail to consider. While critics may object to the social world they imagine home schooled children experience, a careful analysis of traditional schooling raises questions about the experience that children have there as well.

In one of the most insightful and comprehensive studies of home schooling, Milner (2004) and his associates interviewed and observed students at a "typical" American high school. They also reviewed hundreds of essays about life at school that students from across the nation submitted to them. In describing his results, Milner found that the defining feature of high school social life was a hierarchal status system similar to the Indian caste system he had previously studied. In this caste system, social hierarchies and rigid boundaries segregated individuals and groups from each other. Life at school Milner found was comparable. Because of adolescents' marginal status in society and their lack of real decision-making power, one of the few freedoms they had was the power to evaluate each other and to form social hierarchies. Behaviors like who one ate with in the school cafeteria and who one dated and "hung out" with were powerful features of teen social life. Like the Indian caste system, to be seen fraternizing at school with a member of a lower "caste" was threatening to one's status. Thus, rigid boundaries separated students from each other, boundaries that were crossed only at considerable risk, particularly for the higher status student. Cross-boundary interaction was generally acceptable only if it was involuntary such as students assigned to work together on class projects or voluntary if the higher status students were giving the lower status ones a bad time.

In her classic ethnographic study of a Michigan high school, Eckert (1989) found that class distinctions in the larger society reproduce themselves in the relationships that emerge between students at school. She found that school-based peer-groups socially stratify and segregate themselves, and some groups have considerably more power than others. Peer groups often claimed distinct territories at school, wore distinctive clothing, and spoke using a distinctive slang, this to distinguish one group from another.

In his extensive field research of a small Texas town, Foley (1994) found that existing social inequalities are reproduced and reinforced at school through the interaction that occurs there. Foley interviewed Mexican-American and Anglo youth and presented their views of school experiences including relationships with teachers, classroom happenings, sporting events, status hierarchies and the like. He concluded his 14-year research project by concluding that school is an arena where existing values such as individualism and materialism are taught and where students learn to accept their respective positions in society.

In her exploration of school-based adolescent culture, Hersch (1998) found that adolescents live in a world largely invisible to and segregated from adults. Distinct norms and values existed, and drama and crises regularly occurred in the lives of young people that their parents were oblivious to. She writes, "We don't know them. America's own adolescents have become strangers. They are a tribe apart, remote, mysterious, vaguely threatening (p. 14)."

Wiseman (2002) reported that the social world of school-aged girls is both secretive and status oriented. After interviewing hundreds of subjects, Wiseman uncovered the powerful role of cliques and power plays in dictating the behaviors of teenaged girls. Merton (2005) observed a clique of "popular" school girls and found that meanness was a tool they used to maintain both popularity and social boundaries with inclusion and exclusion being important dynamics. Adler, Kless and Adler (1992) conclude their longitudinal observational studies of the school-based youth subculture by reporting that the desire for popularity was a prime motive among young people and that the qualities that produced popularity were gender specific: For males, athletic ability was the prime determinant of popularity followed by social finesse; and for females, physical attractiveness followed by factors related to social class such as nice clothes and homes. Popularity placed students in groups that influenced their opportunities for social interaction and relationships.

For a number of years, I have asked students at the university where I teach to describe in writing their high school experiences. Virtually all describe social hierarchies and the existence of clearly defined groups such as jocks, preps, rednecks, goths, and so on that largely set the parameters for student interaction. Exclusion and social cruelty were the norm.

One of the most striking characteristics of formal education is the age-segregated world that it imposes on young people. Because school children and teens spend so much of their time in relative confinement with same-aged peers, they learn to communicate and develop relationships primarily with them and them alone. One parent wrote in an online conversation:

> I drove around our neighborhood school the other day. One of the reasons I unschool [an unstructured form of home schooling] is because I dislike how society segregates us. Elderly persons are "condemned" to rest homes, adults work, and kids go to school. I looked at that school yard and thought, "How in the world do people expect children to model appropriate adult behavior from being around their peers so much of the time?"

Another striking characteristic of traditional schooling is the segregation that occurs based on race and ethnicity. In the 1954 Brown v. Board of Education of Topeka, Kansas, case, the United States Supreme Court struck down laws mandating racial segregation in public schooling, a practice referred to as de jure (by law) segregation. De facto (in practice) racial segregation, however, remains a major feature of American education where middle- and upper-middle class suburban schools are populated by white and Asian students and inner-city schools are populated with black and Latino students (Orfield 2001). In schools that are racially integrated, most students choose to voluntarily segregate themselves based on race with few cross-racial friendships forming and little cross-racial interaction occurring (Tuch, Sigelman, and McDonald 1999). Most advanced-level courses in integrated schools are dominated by whites and Asians and most of the lower-level classes are dominated by blacks and Latinos (Thernstrom and Thernstrom 2003). This leads to what Kozol (1991, 93) describes as a single school containing within its walls "two separate schools," one for blacks and Latinos, the other for whites and Asians.

I cite these studies to make a point. Despite the potentially restrictive nature of social interaction that some home schooled children experience, critics error in concluding that traditional schools provide a cornucopia of social possibilities. Much of the interaction that happens there is restrictive and sometimes harmful (Olweus 1993). In voicing concern about home schooled children's inability to function in a multicultural world, the text book authors cited earlier implied that public schooled students *have* experiences that allow them to function successfully in such a world, an assumption that has received minimal support from research findings.

Peer dependency is another characteristic of school-based social life. The case has previously been made that youth are highly motivated to belong to social groups and are dependent on them for acceptance and status. Emerson (1981) argues that power is produced by dependency. If we are dependent on others for resources we value such as acceptance and friendship, those we are dependent on have power over us. As a result of this power-dependency dynamic, it is easy to understand the significance of peer dependency and peer-group pressure on traditionally schooled youth who spend so much of their time with same-aged peers. Milner (2004, 4-6) and Wiseman (2002) both found that teens are obsessed with status, and one of the main ways to get it was to conform to the norms of peer culture.

Summarizing these findings leads to the following conclusions about the social life and socialization most students experience at traditional schools: 1) the school-based social world is socially stratified with rigid boundaries segregating students into distinct social groups and limiting their interaction with others; 2) the groups to which students belong consist of friends who tend to be of their same age, social class and race; 3) strict conformity to the norms and values of the youth subculture and group is enforced; 4) inclusion, exclusion, and social cruelty are common; and 5) the social world children and teens experience at school is significantly different from the one they will experience as adults.

These findings do not mean that schooling is a bad experience for all or even most students. Many traditionally schooled students make lifelong friendships, have meaningful relationships with dedicated teachers, master academic skills, and participate in extra-curricular activities that become an important part of their growth and development. Many young people that I know have found traditional schooling to be a positive experience, one that they will look back on in later years with fondness and appreciation. Nevertheless, I have not selectively included only research findings with unfavorable descriptions of life at school in order to defend and justify home schooling. The literature reviewed above is representative of the research in this area and accurately reflects the social realities that exist at traditional schools. The nature of these findings suggests that students, parents, teachers and others should think carefully about school environments and their consequences for the well-being of young people.

Socialization and Home Schooling

In Chapter 1, I wrote that the label "home schooling" was misleading in that it conjured images of children confined to their homes and cut off from the opportunities of the outside world. Consistent with this definition, most home schooling parents I have spoken with chafed at the suggestion that their children were isolated. They believe traditional schools are the places where students are confined and isolated. Ironically, many university students share that sentiment. They have often stated in conversation with me that they look forward to completing their degree programs and then entering the "real world" As these conversations have unfolded, it becomes clear that in their minds college and the real world are separate places.

Parents responded to charges of isolation by highlighting the outside activities that their home schooled children participated in which included boy and girl scouting, 4H, church youth groups, community theatre, community-sponsored athletic teams, library-based reading groups, music, dance, and martial arts lessons, penpals, part-time jobs and volunteering. In some of the larger cities throughout the United States, parents, teens and children have organized home school-based orchestras, bands, sports teams, theatrical productions, proms, parties, internships of various kinds, summer camps and graduation ceremonies complete with caps and gowns.

Most home school critics that I have spoken with assume that traditional school settings are the only places where viable social opportunities present themselves to young people. In other words, if children aren't having worthwhile social experiences at school, they aren't having them at all. The home school movement rejects that assumption and research findings on the topic support their beliefs. Two independent reviews of the literature on home schooling and socialization both found that home schooled children have meaningful relationships, are integrated into their communities, and have the necessary knowledge and skills to function effectively in society (McDowell 2004; Medlin 2000).

Ray (1997, 77-8) reports that home schooled children spent significant amounts of time playing with children outside their families and were involved in community-based activities while they spent little time playing computer games and watching television. Medlin (1998) finds that home schooled children interact on a regular basis with a diverse array of people outside their families including people of diverse ages, socio-economic backgrounds and the like. Rudner (1999) in a study of 20,760 home schooled students from 11,930 families who align themselves with the Christian Right, finds support for the belief that these youth are academically successful as measured by their scores on standardized tests. Consistent with Ray's study, he finds that home schooled children watch considerably less television the do traditionally schooled children and there is no evidence that they cannot function successfully in society. Chaplin-Carpenter (1994) asked both home and traditionally schooled students to keep records of all people they interacted with for an entire month. She finds when comparing contacts with diverse people, the differences between home and traditionally schooled students are not statistically significant. This meant that although the traditionally schooled students in her study had slightly more contacts with others than did home schooled students, 56 to 49 contacts, respectively, that difference likely resulted from sampling error. In other words, traditionally and home schooled students have comparable numbers of contacts with diverse people.

In perhaps the most rigorous study on home schooling and social adjustment to date, Shyers (1992) compared 70 home schooled children with 70 traditionally schooled children. Shyers matched the groups based on age, social class, number of siblings, involvement outside the home and other relevant variables. These groups of children 8 to 10 years of age were videotaped on two separate occasions while engaging in structured and unstructured activities respectively. Using a double-blind design (Babbie 2005, 232-3), trained observers who did not know that the groups consisted of traditional and home schooled students watched the videos and rated the behaviors of the children in each group using an established and respected instrument designed for that purpose. Compared with the traditionally schooled students, the home schooled students exhibited superior interpersonal skills. For example, Shyers found that the traditionally schooled students were much more aggressive and uncooperative than the home schooled group who were friendlier, easier going and more cooperative.

Because of the quality of Shyers' design including the matching of subjects, the double-blind component which eliminated any possibility that the preconceptions of the observers toward home and traditional schooling biased their evaluations, and the instrumentation which ensured reliability, these results are considered solid. They provide support for the belief that home schooled children are well-adjusted and have adequate interpersonal skills. While research studies on home schooling are of uneven quality largely because of problems associated with sampling and generalization, the consistency in findings offers support for the belief that home schooling is a positive social experience for most children. My observations over the past decade support these conclusions. I see no evidence that home schooled children, as a collective, are isolated, anti-social, maladjusted, or lacking in interpersonal skills. All the home schooled graduates I know seem to be living relatively conventional, well-adjusted lives as adults. Very few of them reported being resentful of home schooling, most found it to be a positive experience, and some plan to home school their own children. My findings concur with Knowles and Muchmore (1995, 35) who concluded their study of adults who were home schooled as children by stating that they are "doing just fine."

As Medlin (2000) concluded his review of the literature on socialization and home schooling, he listed some quality control concerns that included "no guiding theory, inadequate experimental design, poorly defined research questions, untried and weak measures, unorthodox treatment and presentation of data, and conclusions based on subjective judgments" (p. 118). Finally, he worried about the reliability of self-reported questionnaire data often used in this research. I agree with his critique and add my own concerns about the lack of adequate sampling frames and low response rates common in the questionnaire-based research on home schooling. I worry most, however, about the tendency of zealous home schoolers to herald the results of these studies without an awareness of their shortcomings. Home school advocates, of course, are not the only ones who do this. Researchers throughout the academic world, mindful of the limitations in their research, state their findings with the proper caution and nuance while partisans in their enthusiasm to advance their own particular agendas, combined with their ignorance of research methodologies, throw caution to the wind and over-generalize the results.

As one who is a consumer of research studies, I must emphasize that concerns like the ones listed above are not unique to the literature on home schooling. Many studies rely on self-reported data, have sampling problems of one kind or another, are inadequately designed and lack theoretical grounding. Few research studies are without flaw. Despite these problems, the consistency of the findings of the studies cited here is reassuring and to at least some extent mutes these methodological concerns. The overwhelming number of studies that explored socialization and home schooling concluded that it is a positive experience for children.

Dangerous Minds

In reply to my colleague's concern that fanatical parents could use home schooling to impose dangerous view on their children, I acknowledge that this does on occasion happen. Two examples come to mind. First, a network news website carried a story about a pair of female teenaged siblings who have gained fame and notoriety by performing and recording songs that cater to the white supremacy movement. The teens' mother uses home schooling to indoctrinate her daughters with the philosophy and values of neo-Nazism including the belief in the supremacy of the white race and in denying the holocaust.

Second, one of my students who is a home schooling parent wrote a paper for a class assignment in which she quoted a speech given by a man at a home school convention she attended (Repp 2005). The speaker, a religious fundamentalist, lauded home schooling as a tool for dominating his family and for ensuring that worldly influences did not corrupt them. He expressed particular concern about his wife and daughter and was grateful for the control that home schooling provided him and for the consequences of that control in their lives. He stated:

> My wife regrets the independence that was cultivated in her own life when she got a driver's license. This is an area we've chosen to avoid for our daughter. It's not that long ago historically that driving was considered something women should leave to men. If Mary's husband, when she marries, wants her to get a driver's license, that'll be up to him. But we've decided not to rob *him* [emphasis added] of that decision. Mary is grateful for the protection from such seemingly innocent influences toward independence. (p. 7)

Regarding the white supremacists, home school critics may be quick to suggest that if the singers attended a public school they would have influences in their lives that would counteract their mother's ideology and thus lead them to hold more tolerant world views. While possible, I believe a less optimist outcome is at least as likely, that being one where tension and conflict at their school increases due to their behaviors and attitudes with no decrease in their offensive ways. Given that a host of white supremacists including skin heads, neo-Nazis and others have attended traditional schools, the hope that schooling would eradicate or even minimize racist beliefs is in my view naive. As Holt (1981) argued:

> Even if we all agreed that the schools should try to stamp out narrow and bigoted ideas, we would still have to ask ourselves, does this work? Clearly it doesn't.
> After all, except for a few rich kids almost all children in the country have been going to public schools now for several generations. If the schools were as good as they claim at stamping out prejudice, there ought not to be any left. A quick glance at today's news will show that there is plenty left. (p. 42)

In regard to the controlling father, I suspect that traditional schooling would to some extent counter his sexist ideology. The dreadfulness of his statement with its Taliban-style view of gender roles reveals itself in layers, and home schooling organized as a total institution (Goffman 1961) would be necessary to produce people in general and females in particular who would conform to those views. This raises a question asked years ago by Holt (1981). Even if the government and its schools could stamp out bad ideas and replace them with good ones, should they do so? He asked:

> Suppose we decided to give the government the power, through compulsory schools, to promote good ideas and put down bad. To whom would we then give the power to decide *which* ideas were good and which bad? To legislatures? To state school boards? To local school boards? Anyone who thinks seriously about these questions will surely agree that no one in government should have such power. (p. 41)

Holt argued that in a free society people must be free to believe as they choose and to pass those beliefs on to their children. He acknowledged that bigoted and prejudiced parents will teach their views to their children but he asks "what is the alternative?" The answer is totalitarianism.

How Much is Too Much

One question these findings raise involves the optimal level of participation of children and teens in organized activities outside their home and family. Parents in general have tended to enroll their children in increasing numbers of these activities (Adler and Adler 1994) including home schooling parents (Delahooke 1986; Montgomery 1989; Ray 1997). What remains unknown is how much involvement in outside social activities is necessary for the optimal well-being of children and teens. Most parents I know have a "more is better" mindset and encourage their children to participate in a substantial number of such activities with some home schooling parents, eager to prove that their children are not isolated, enrolling them in even more. Some critics, however, have raised questions about these "over-scheduled" children and have urged parents to scale back (Rosenfeld and Wise 2001). They suggest a more simplified life with fewer activities serves children better.

In a beautifully written essay, Price (2001), a novelist and university professor, described the generous amounts of solitude he was "blessed" to experience as a child in the woods near his family's summer home, and the benefits solitude had for both his personal development and for his success as an adult. His time playing alone in the woods allowed him to develop both his imagination and his own unique identity. The university students he teaches who had peer-saturated childhoods are qualitatively different. He observed:

> In the students I teach at a first-rate university today, I notice the triumph of a disturbing herd mentality . . . When I contemplate the near-paralyzing addiction to company and the fear of solitude that drive so many Americans today, I feel hugely grateful for the thousands of solitary summer days in my childhood. (p. 73)

Louv (2005) laments the diminished amounts of time children spend in unstructured outdoor play and the increases in time they spend with the electronic media and in adult-directed activities. He believes this has contributed to a host of problems including attention deficit hyperactivity disorder, depression, stress and anxiety problems. The antidote for these problems he believes is a return to the childhood Price described. Kerr (1985) explored the personal lives of successful women such as Marie Curie, Gertrude Stein, Eleanor Roosevelt, Margaret Mead, and Maya Angelou. She found that they were often alone, but that they used solitude to their advantage and forged strong independent selves. Although the evidence for solitude (as opposed to isolation) is largely poetic and anecdotal, I believe it deserves attention from social and behavioral scientists and that it is a possible remedy for the over-socialized, crowded world many traditional and home schooled youth inhabit.

Conclusions

In summarizing these research findings, the evidence suggests that traditional schools, in general, do not provide children with the universally positive social experience some imagine while home schooling, in general, is not the isolating experience some fear. Both have strengths and weaknesses. A balanced view is necessary as each offers a legitimate and necessary alternative to members of a pluralistic society.

5
Doubts and Fears

Do I dare
disturb the universe?
T.S. Eliot, from The Love Song of J. Alfred Prufrock

One of sociology's most important insights is that people can easily internalize the "official versions" society offers without a second thought. It's easy to walk down the well-worn paths of cultural habits without heeding Bellah and his colleague's (1991) plea to "pay attention" and ask thoughtful questions about what's going on around us. Good citizenship, they believe, requires us to develop an awareness of the social and cultural forces that shape our lives and yet all too often become so routine, so taken for granted, that we fail to give them the scrutiny they deserve. Questioning official versions and taking the road less traveled can be a rewarding, yet stressful ,experience.

An Unsettled Life

Violating social conventions can produce anxiety, a reoccurring companion of most home school parents that I know, particularly new home schooling parents. As Guterson (1998) stated:

> When they speak in public, home-schooling parents often appear confident, answer detractors defiantly and are bold in the criticisms of schools. But privately they often wonder whether they're making a huge mistake. This doubt, I think, is part and parcel of the undertaking, central to its definition. School teachers feel some variant of it, too. To educate is to be terrified at the enormity and importance of the task. (p. 71)

While I like Guterson's quote, I accept it only with a minor revision. Many home schooling parents I know do suffer from the anxiety he describes, but few teachers or professors that I know do. Most of my contemporaries work hard, are committed to education and care about their students. These same contemporaries, however, seldom, if ever, question the structure of education itself. Traditional classrooms, textbooks, ringing bells, multiple-choice tests, lectures and note-taking are assumed without a second thought.

This is not to say that teachers and professors don't have fleeting doubts about their efficacy or that they don't develop varying degrees of cynicism about their students or the educational bureaucracy that is the structure their work lives. But they seldom question the very structure of formal education and the assumptions upon which it rests because it is so routine and accepted. Because home schooling parents are marching to the beat of a different drummer, they do not experience the emotional protection that conformity offers, and they are left to negotiate identities in a world suspicious of their views. Anxiety, defined as discomfort, worry and fear that people experience about what may happen given a course of action they have chosen is often their frequent companion. How it is both produced and managed will be explored in this chapter. To understand the relationship between the identities home schooling families negotiate and their relationship with the anxiety they experience, the sociological approach to the development of the self concept must be briefly explored because I believe that some of the processes that influence its development also influence anxiety.

Gecas (1982, 10) stated, "If there is a central theme in the sociological literature on the self-concept it is the idea that the content and organization of self-concepts reflect the content and organization of society." In other words, people are influenced by the structure of the society in which they live and the definitions of reality members of that society share, definitions that are communicated through interaction. Citing Rosenburg (1979), Gecas argued that scholars must go "beyond" self concept as self esteem to self concept as identity which was defined in Chapter 4 as a negotiated settlement between a person and others as to who that person is. Gecas argued for:

> [T]he social situation as the context in which identities are established and maintained through the process of negotiation. The identity negotiation . . . is a central aspect of the individual's broader task of "defining the situation" and "constructing reality." (p. 10)

The definition of home schooling collectively held by the broader society will, therefore, influence the identities and social relationships of home schooling families for good or ill. Identities are negotiated through social interaction via two processes: 1) reflected appraisals and 2) social comparisons.

Reflected Appraisals

In 1902, Cooley created a theoretic construct he labeled the Looking Glass Self as an explanation for the development of the human self (reprinted in O'Brien 2006, 255-57). This explanation describes an identity as being constructed through interaction with others in a three-step process: 1) a person imagines how he or she is viewed by others; 2) as that person interacts with others, he or she receives and interprets "reflections" from them as to what kind of person he or she is; and 3) that person internalizes those reflections, and they become a part of his or her identity. In sum, the people we interact with serve as a looking glass of sorts and "reflect back to us" information that we use to define ourselves. Are we worthy or unworthy, wise or foolish, strong or weak, attractive or unattractive, competent or incompetent, and so on?

Consider a young school girl who is very attractive and smart. Everyone admires her and, as she interacts with others, positive reflections are the norm. Adults are complimentary of the things she says, other girls her age want to be her friend. Compare this girl's situation with the plight of a less attractive school girl who struggles with a learning disability. The feedback she receives from others is often negative and hurtful. Over time, the reflected appraisals these individuals receive will have a powerful, cumulative effect on both their identities. Granted, the interpretive process described in step two is not always accurate as people often misinterpret the reflections of others, but the process is strong nonetheless.

The relevance of Cooley's ideas for home schooling is important. As parents and children consider home schooling and as their careers in home schooling unfold, the feedback they receive from others has an enormous impact on them and on the levels of anxiety they experience. If "significant others" and casual acquaintances alike question their decision and treat them with ridicule and suspicion, this can change their identities and alter their relationships. As Goffman (1959) argued, people are highly motivated to manage the impressions that others have of them. If they fail in this undertaking, they lose face, one of the most negative and stressful outcomes humans experience. The public image of home schooling plays a big part here.

While home schooling has achieved a degree of respectability and while open confrontation with authorities has of late been minimized (Knowles, Marlow and Muchmore 1992), many members of society remain ambivalent and suspicious of this practice. This ambivalence reveals itself in media depictions of home schooling both real (1-3 below) and fictitious (4-5): 1) a young Texas mother pushed to the brink by mental illness, religious extremism, isolation and home schooling drowns all five of her children; 2) Tennessee parents shielded by the invisibility home schooling offered subjected their children to years of horrific physical and emotional abuse; 3) survivalists in Northern Idaho home schooled their children while they stockpiled arms in anticipation of Armageddon; 4) the hit movie *Mean Girls* opens with a depiction of home schooled children as "freaks" who are either nerdy spelling bee winners or bible-thumping, gun-totting rednecks; and 5) in a recent Dean Koontz (2006) best seller, the protagonist's parents use home schooling to impose a Skinnerian hell on their children. In a place labeled the "learning room," the children become lab rats of sorts who are used to test their father's psychological theories turning one of them into a monster and leaving permanent scares on the rest.

So long as this ambivalence and suspicion remain, home schooling families will continue to receive unsettling reflected appraisals from others, appraisals that can increase the levels of anxiety they experience. A recent home school graduate told me, "Many of my friends and relatives were hostile to the idea of home schooling at first. It was a fairly new idea a lot of people felt threatened." In a letter to me another wrote:

> I distinctly remember laying in a hammock in my front yard watching the neighborhood kids catch the school bus across the street, and yelling out "illiterate" to me as they went past. This didn't bother me, since I figured they had probably just learned a new word and wanted to try it out, and if they had any sense they would have looked and seen two volumes of Dickens beside me. I was nine at the time.

While it's easy for people to say that the verbal slings and arrows hurled by others don't hurt, this woman vividly remembers these experiences years later suggesting they were notable experiences in her life. Mistrust of home schooling on a personal level is often enhanced by characteristics of individual families. If families appears organized, bright, and respectable, the decision to home school will be easier for significant others to tolerate. In our case, few people openly criticized our decision. My Ph.D. and professorial profession combined with Ranae's college degree and years of experience as a piano teacher didn't hurt our case as we knew other less credentialized individuals who had more acceptance troubles then we did.

A mother described the experience of catching someone "drilling" her children to prove they were being poorly educated:

> Today I walked my two daughters and their cousin and her friend to a general store . . . When the cousin and friend thought I was out of earshot they started drilling Susan on fractions, of all things. Susan did fairly well-she's more confident about these attacks by her peers then she used to be,but I told the girls, "I know you get to drill Susan and Heather about Fractions,and I will drill you about World War II, Ready? Their jaws dropped and the cousin said, "We don't learn about history until the sixth grade." Enough said.

A home school graduate wrote me about how people would drill her with questions, and she shared her humorous reactions to them:

> I had some people grill me about my education, like the cashier at the local grocery store. They would drill questions at a little ten year old girl—What school? Where is it? What are the school colors? And so on, an endless stream. Some people, immediately upon finding out I was home schooled, decided that

my parents took me out because I either stupid or disabled. Then I got long, sympathetic monologues about how happy they were for me, coated in sugar and syrup. I think the worst ones were the ones who reacted as though you were some kind of religious zealot or communist, depending on the person's outlook. This resulted in a sermon my direction. All of them were useless, and sometimes cruel for a child.

The interesting thing is that as a home schooler of the old guard, I can tell you a little secret about dealing with these people. The best way to deal with them is always to feed on their fears. Not only does it relieve any pressure on you, it always leaves the person confused. For we few home schoolers it became a game. To quote a scripture to the left, and Marx to the right. My favorite was always to play dumb with the ones who grilled you like well-trained police detectives. What school do you go to? *I don't remember*. Where is it? *It's around here somewhere*. Shuffle your feet and shake your head. That sort of thing. We also like to have long discussions about Shakespeare or something lofty (which we knew very little about at that age) in front of the "stupid people." It may sound petty or dangerous now, but then it just felt like self defense.

Often home schooling parents sought out friends who supported them and their children in their decision and provided positive appraisals. Social networks changed as hostile relationships were replaced with supportive ones, not unlike the transitions that occur when people change their religion or experience some other significant transformation. The more parents interacted with like-minded people, the more assured they were in what they were doing and the less anxiety they experienced. Consequently, home school support groups were very popular among new home school parents in my study. A mother posted the following comments to an online home school support group we belonged to shortly after she began home schooling. Her comments reflect the fear she felt as she entered unchartered waters and the reassurance she received from the group.

I'm just fearful of the authorities telling me that I just not doing things right. Gosh, I feel practically phobic about failing on this my greatest project: my children. Ive just come up against such adverse reaction from friends about my wanting to home school that I'm a little insecure. Thank goodness for all of you. . . I am beginning to feel a little normal.

Negative reflected appraisals are powerful forces in people's lives. They influence the identities people develop as well as the relationships they form and maintain.

Social Comparisons

In addition to reflected appraisals, identities are formed based on comparisons made with others. People make comparisons involving their appearance, intelligence, popularity, education level, careers, possessions, personal and family accomplishments and so on. Parents are, of course, notorious for their tendency to compare their children with other children and to get social mileage out of their children's victories and shame out of their defeats. The people we interact with provide an evaluative frame of reference that we use to form conclusions about ourselves and others. Home schooling families are no different. Outside the protection of the mainstream, the parents in my study were more vulnerable to the influence of comparisons. Even the most strident unschoolers who reject social definitions of education know that they will be held responsible for their children's education. In their hearts, most will hold themselves responsible as well. *If a child attends public school and can't read, it's the school's fault. If a child is home schooled and can't read, it's the parents fault.* Aware of this pressure, home schooling parents wonder if they are up to it. A parent stated, "Mark quit public schooling in March of last year. He had a miserable experience. I hung on as long as I did because I felt inadequate to educate him myself."

This mother realized that her child was floundering in a traditional school with no relief in sight but she questioned her ability to provide him with an adequate education. She continued the conversation by comparing her training and the resources she could provide with that offered by traditional schools. She doubted she could measure up. Another mother, just two weeks into home schooling her young children, emailed Ranae a message with the following concerns:

> I just don't know. Will the kids really learn enough? What will my in laws say? Tomorrow I could put them back in school and no one the wiser. I will stress out over this tonight. What am I doing to myself? Will it really pay off in the long run? Will the house ever be quiet again? Will they really learn to do what I ask? Will the house ever be clean again?

Uncertainty and worry weighed on her mind. Her struggle pitted her convictions about what was best for her children against her fear that she would fail them, a failure that would have an added depth to it because she would lose face in the eyes of her family. She worried about her ability to adjust to the added workload. She also expressed concern about family reunions and other gatherings where high-achieving cousins who attended traditional schools would overshadow her credential-less children.

Discussions about inspiring teachers, unique and challenging courses, foreign exchange programs, field trips, proms, sports teams, and other experiences home schooled children may miss can produce both stress and second thoughts in parents. Several friends and relatives of ours regularly discussed the happenings in their children's school lives. These were dear friends who were merely informing us of the accomplishments of their children with no intention of showing us up or undermining our confidence, but sometimes unknowingly did anyway. These discussions produced more anxiety and second guessing in me than anything else. Some home schooling families withdrew from threatening relationships and steered clear of negative people. A seasoned home schooling parent informed others of what many of them could expect from some acquaintances.

> At first you have to put up with all sorts of little ploys from family and friends protesting about how the kids will not be socialized, they won't learn

anything, and how can you possibly think you're smart enough to teach them. It gets to you after a while but you've got to move on.

If the criticism comes from someone emotionally close, it is all the more difficult, more difficult still if it comes from one's spouse. A woman reflected on her experiences as she anticipated her first day of home schooling her enthusiastic daughters. She thought she had the support of her husband only to have him change his mind at the last minute.

> We had talked about home schooling for so long, and most of this school year we have looked at it as something to get ready to do it. Then Pete tells us "No!" I am torn between anger and rage and heartbreaking sadness. He has to go on to say he doesn't think we can teach them enough, or teach them well.

The woman felt insulted and betrayed by her husband's reversal and authoritarian manner: *It doesn't matter what you think, you will not home school our children.* Granted, this is an issue where honest people can and will have strong opinions. The example above is no different than the cases I've known where the mother home schools the children against the father's wishes.

Among the people I've known, spousal/partner disagreement on the issue generally revolved around whether or not children would learn more in traditional schools and have better experiences compared with what home schooling could provide. This concern was often offensive to the mother who interpreted her husband's concerns as an affront to her abilities and intelligence. The children were of course aware of the parent discord on this issue and this undermined their motivation and confidence as well. I have not known a single case where fathers and mothers were deeply divided on home schooling where the attempt at it was successful and not soon abandoned. Needless to say, spousal divisiveness on this issue was a major source of stress among some home schooling mothers.

In all of these cases, contention about children's education approached and even surpassed the contention in some marriages about whose faith the children will be raised in. Unlike many conventional issues that couples traditionally discuss before marriage and parenthood (i.e. money, religion, careers and childcare), home schooling was something new and unexpected that emerged after the children were born. As a growing numbers of home school graduates enter adulthood, and as they and others inclined towards home schooling contemplate parenthood, this will likely become a major issue for them and their partners to resolve before having children. The educational choices of home schooled graduates will also be an important topic of investigation for future research.

Another form of anxiety-producing comparisons occurs between home schooling families and the idealized image of home schooling offered by advocacy groups and organizations. Using samples drawn from non-representative segments of the home school population, some proponents have created an image of home schooling that is both inaccurate and impossible for many to achieve. Relying on families who use Bob Jones University Testing and Evaluation Service, Rudner

(1999), for example, reported that respondents scored in the 70-80 percentile on standardized tests. What was obscured in the reporting of his findings was the non-representative nature of his sample and the sweeping conclusions that have been inappropriately drawn from it (Welner and Welner 1999).

In another highly publicized study of the academic achievement of home schooled students, Ray (1977) found they scored in the 87th percentile on the Iowa Test of Basic Skills. However, Ray acknowledges problems with the sample and the response rate. In the published report, Ray states that a response rate between 28.8 and 41 percent was achieved, but he has no way of knowing exactly what it was. Even if the rate was 41 percent, it remains problematic and raises a host of concerns about both the sample and the results. First, due to personal desirability issues, students with high test scores may have been more likely to return surveys than students who did not score well. Second, many home schoolers refuse to participate in survey research projects. Those who refuse to participate may be different in a variety of ways from those who chose to participate. Third, the home school movement is politically divided and the organization that Ray used to distribute the questionnaires is disliked and distrusted by many home school families, many of whom would have been unlikely to either receive questionnaires or return them if they received them.

Fourth, many home school families reject standardized tests as invalid and unreliable measures of learning and refuse to take them. Finally, significant evidence suggests a relationship between socio-economic class, family stability, and standardized test scores, with middle- and upper-class students from two-parent families scoring higher on standardized tests than lower-income students. Given that home schooling is a middle-class, two-parent family phenomenon, this raises the possibility that home schooled students would have scored just as high on these tests had they been enrolled in traditional schools. Controls need to be employed in any comparison of scores before conclusions can be drawn about the causal effect of home schooling on standardized test scores. The most that can be said about this study and others like it is that the students who chose to return questionnaires seem to have achieved impressive scores on these tests. The implication left by my reading of this report was that the 87th percentile ranking is typical of home schooled children in general, an implication I believe is unwarranted and inaccurate.

I know disillusioned and disheartened ex-home schoolers who abandoned the practice when unrealistic expectations suggested by these and other findings could not be met. I also fear that trumpeting results such as these sets home schooling up for a fall when critics learn that many home schooled children do not achieve scores as high as these findings suggest.

Antidotes for Anxiety

While reflected appraisals and social comparisons often produce anxiety, successful families manage anxiety and maintain confidence through the following: 1) support and resolve within the family for home schooling; 2) support and reassurance from fellow home schoolers and other supportive people; 3) reflecting on positive home schooling experiences and outcomes; 4) continued rejection of traditional schooling; 5) redefining education, socialization and family life in ways sympathetic to home schooling; and 6) the growing societal acceptance of home schooling.

Support, cohesion and resolve within the family for home schooling are the most important sources of anxiety reduction. Lois (2006) found that as mothers launched their home schooling careers, they were often overwhelmed by the added workload associated with it. She found that a major antidote for the resulting burnout was the support these women received from their husbands. My research supports Lois's findings and adds the importance of positive and supportive relationships between mothers and their children.

Teaching children in a home schooling environment against their will was very problematic. Granted, traditional schools have dealt with uncooperative students for decades. The family dimension inherent in home schooling, however, complicated the situation because the roles of parent, sibling, teacher and classmate are blended. Home can be a haven for students who struggle at school, but because school and home are the same place for the children in my study, problems sometimes arose.

Home schooling can be a good thing, but the odds of success increase if all family members are supportive and have arrived at a consensus that it is the right thing to do. This is not to say that even in the best of situations conflicts won't occur and challenges won't emerge that need to be overcome. While all families have their share of these difficulties, they are more salient for home schooling families because of the continued physical proximity and intensity of the structure of their relationships. Successful families develop both emotional cohesion and share a commitment to home schooling.

Affirmation from other home schoolers and other sympathetic people does much to reduce anxiety and build confidence. I remember one colleague at work who regularly complimented me on our decision and the benefits he was sure would come our way because of it. My conversations with him were welcome and reassuring. This support, however, is more important during the first few years of the home schooling experience when families are inexperienced, are adjusting to a new lifestyle, and negotiating new identities. It is also during the early years when reactions from family and friends are likely to be the most strident. After my subjects had been at it for a while and assumed the identity of home schoolers, it became easier. The significant others in their lives had time to deal with them and to adjust to the reality that home schooling is a part of their relative's or friend's life. They often learn to either accept the decision at best or leave it alone at worst. Consequently, most persistent home schoolers receive diminishing amount of criticism from relatives and friends as time passes.

The first year or two, we felt a real need to join a home school support group. This group was composed of other new home schooling families as well. We supported each other in our respective decisions to home school, shared ideas, discussed common challenges, planned field trips and socials, and griped about past experiences in the public schools. The group filled a need, namely acceptance, support, and friendship as we sailed in an unchartered sea. The group dissolved after a few years when members felt more comfortable with their decision, improved their skills, developed other priorities, moved away, or abandoned home schooling.

Reflecting on positive home schooling experiences and outcomes is another technique of anxiety reduction. There must be successes and good times for home schools to persist. As with any other endeavor, the ability to savor successful moments—listening to a child read her first sentence, read an insightful essay a child has written, or experience a special moment when you connect with your child, must be developed and enjoyed. Experiences such as these allay fears, suggest success, and provide beacons of hope when times get tough.

Several families come to mind who abandoned home schooling when there were no perceived successes. The decision to persist, like most decisions, is often based on some type of cost benefit analysis and unless the benefits exceed the costs, families are unlikely to continue home schooling. One parent noted the increased tension in her home as she tried to be both parent and teacher. Another felt overwhelmed and exhausted as well as being frustrated at her supposed inability to influence her children to accomplish worthwhile educational goals. Still another didn't see any appreciable results of any kind and noted added stress in the family. Those who persist find it rewarding. I maintain that once a family begins home schooling, something good has to happen reasonably soon. Home schooling families are swimming upstream as it is.

Some of our successes were seeing our children selecting good books without be prodded, acquiring new skills, and developing unique tastes in music. While our sons have all experienced reasonable levels of academic success, the major benefit of home sc hooling for us has been manifest in their characters and in our relationships with them. While there are undoubtedly school experiences they have missed, the youth subculture has not had the hold on them that it would have had.

Another antidote for anxiety is the continued rejection of formal schooling. This rejection involved remembering bad experiences at school and interacting with others who define traditional schooling in a negative way. This shared "definition of the situation" reinforced their resolve to home school and provided a common enemy of sorts. Melucci (1989) argued that social movement members must interact with those who define their personal distress in a way consistent with the aims of the movement. Support groups serve that purpose. The home school movement began as a reaction to and rejection of traditional schools. Critics became convinced that the institutionalized life traditional schools offered harmed children and that alternatives were needed (Bennett 1972; Illich 1971). Home schooling emerged as perhaps the most successful alternative to traditional schooling as proponents articulated careful and convincing justifications for it (Colfax and Colfax 1988; Guterson 1992; Holt 1981; Llewellyn 1991). The generally negative image of public schools in the media contributed to the definition of schools as bad places and to home schooling as a promising alternative. Some of the guarded acceptance the home school movement has experienced is because of concerns the public has about public schools.

Despite my support of home schooling, combined with my concerns about traditional schools, I believe that segments of the home school movement should exercise more restraint in their attacks on public schools. While I've already raised concerns about the inappropriate generalizations of research on the academic success of home schooling, demonizing public schools can be counterproductive as well. Some critics go so far as to argue that public schools should be abolished and be replaced with alternatives like home schooling (Gatto 2002; Richman 1995). These arguments are extreme, unrealistic and divisive. The majority of contemporary parents are not in a position to implement home schooling even if they believed it's the right thing to do which of course they don't. They rely on public schools. Consequently, overly combative posturing on public schooling will drive wedges between the home school movement and the general public whose support they need.

I have listened to numerous speeches and read many pamphlets and books calling for the demise of public education in the harshest of terms. I cannot imagine anything good coming of these attacks. Some critics have told me they await with great anticipation the collapse of public schooling and they are sure home schooling can take up the slack. That belief is absurd. Home schooling could never take up the slack of a collapsed education system. If members of the home school movement want the respect of the larger society for the educational decisions they have made, they must give it back in return.

Redefining education, socialization and family life in ways sympathetic to home schooling is another anecdote. The unstructured approach to home schooling labeled unschooling has redefined education. Education, they argue, is not something that occurs in confined classrooms as a student labors over material deemed important to someone else. Knowledge is not measured by standardized tests that reduce the educational experience (and often the worth of a student) to a score or a percentile ranking. Learning takes place when people are placed in environments free of fear (i.e. tests, peer groups, etc.) where curiosity and personal interest are the prime motivators and learning for the joy of learning is the process. If learning can be measured at all, it is measured by the joy one feels as he or she engages in the learning process. In sum, anxiety is reduced if traditional educational definitions are rejected and replaced by others that both legitimize home schooling and present a different view of learning.

Some unschoolers I know are fond of the statement, a statement they directed at the school-at-home crowd: Don't try to out school, school. By this, they mean home schools should not try to do a better job of formal schooling, than formal schools. If parents are going to impose formal schooling at home, they might just as well send their children to school. Rather, a different educational paradigm should guide home schools. That paradigm is that an unstructured, child-directed educational plan where natural curiosity is the guiding light is the best way to educate children.

The structured school-at-home segment of the home school movement is not defenseless in this debate. They argue that a customized formal educational plan freed from the influences of the youth subculture offers an outstanding educational experience. They emphasize the custom nature of their curricula, the tutoring they offer their children, the relationships that are built, and the values that are instilled. The relationships and values are more important to most of the school-at-home people that I know than the credentials offered at public or private schools.

Home schooling is as much a lifestyle as it is an educational choice. Perhaps more than anything else, it requires a redefinition of family life. Home schooling is an attempt to establish the family as a true primary social group. Home schooling involves a rejection of the post-modern family with its dual careers, 60-70-hour work weeks for both parents and excessive after-school activities.

The growing societal acceptance of home schooling is a final anecdote for anxiety that I will discuss here. Typical of many successful social movements, social movement pioneers are often considered extremists by mainstream society. Consider the Civil Rights Movement and the Women's Movement as notable examples of this phenomenon. Early feminists and Civil Rights leaders were considered oddballs and malcontents. After much work and with the passage of time, they became respectable. Although still marginal, the home school movement has gained some respectability. When we began home schooling our sons many years ago, some people treated us as an oddity. Today the number of raised eyebrows has diminished. Some even seem warm to the idea and compliment us on our choice.

A growing number of public institutions acknowledge home schooling. Some public libraries have home school appreciation days. Some museums we have visited extend the same educational discounts to home school families as they do to public school students. Our home school student body card produced the same discount at our local movie theater as does a public school student body card. All of the public schools in my state invite home schooled children to enroll in classes part time and to participate, to a limited extent, in extra-curricular activities. Although controversial and ironic, most states offer online public schooling to home schooled families via online schools. These virtual public schools generally provide computers, textbooks, online courses, socials, graduation ceremonies and credentials such as report cards and diplomas. My auto insurance company, a major national insurance firm, accepted our home school report card for the good student discount. As a result of recent legislation, all branches of the armed services accept home schooled graduates without requiring them to get a General Education Development (GED) certificate. Military academies offer qualified home school graduates the possibility of admission as well.

Most universities have changed their admissions policies to accommodate home schooling to at least some extent. This they have done for at least two reasons: First, home school graduates have performed well in college. Second, and perhaps most importantly, there is fierce competition among universities for students. With ever-increasing numbers of home schooled students graduating each year, a market has been created that colleges and universities hungry for increased headcounts will never ignore. While in days gone by, higher education viewed home school applications with suspicion and concern, some universities are rallying to recruit home schooled students. This grants legitimacy to the home school movement by neutralizing one of the major fears that home school families faced in the past: "What about college?"

In summary, while home schooling remains on the margins and positive identities are not always easy to negotiate, a variety of strategies help minimize the anxiety associated with this educational and lifestyle choice. As the collective position of home schooling has improved, students are currently offered a variety of opportunities they were previously denied.

6
Challenging Assumptions

*No social study that does not come back to the problem of biography,
of history and of their intersections within a society has completed
its intellectual journey Mills (2005, 14).*

History and Biography

In order to understand the appeal and existence of home schooling in contemporary society and to place it in its proper social context, a number of social phenomena must be understood. While I made it clear earlier in this book that I would not dwell on these issues, a brief discussion is in order.

First, sociologists have written about the alienation and powerlessness that people experience in societies dominated by large formal organizations such as government agencies, global corporations, the medical establishment, the electronic media, and mass education. By their very nature, formal organizations are motivated to survive and grow, to not only maintain but also expand their power and influence; but while they attempt this expansion and intrude on the lives of people, resentment and resistance can sometimes result (Habermas 1981).

Second, in response to this discontent, alternative means of satisfying basic human needs emerge. These alternatives emerge as a result of the collective behavior of people who join together, organize themselves, mobilize resources, seek to overcome resistance from established interests and often to seek recruits. Examples of this include home schooling, alternative medicine, and new political parties. While the growth of these alternatives is in part a testament to the loss of confidence that people have in formal organizations and institutions, I believe they represent something more, namely the desire for personal empowerment and self reliance; a need to feel in control of one's life and family in the face of mass society. That home schooling has counterparts that have emerged in response to other major social institutions demonstrates the widespread and powerful nature of the momentum of which home schooling is but a part.

The alternative health movement provides a good example of the phenomenon (Schneirov and Geezik 1996). The eclectic mixture of people who participate in this movement consist of conservative Christians, libertarians, progressives, and members of the new age movement-a population not unlike many home schoolers I know. Many alternative health participants reported negative experiences with conventional health care institutions. Some complained that they were mistreated and depersonalized. My reading of this research is that in order to understand the lure of the alternative health movement, one must look beyond the efficacy of the remedies it prescribes to the larger issue looming beyond, that of the desire for personal autonomy.

Home schoolers, likewise, place a premium on the values of autonomy and self reliance. Home schooling can, in part, be viewed as a rejection of what has been called the "age of the expert," the increasingly widespread tendency of many to cede control of their lives to "experts." Classical sociologist Emile Durkheim (1961) wrote about the division of labor that occurs in industrial and postindustrial societies where the activities of people become so specialized that they lose many of the skills those in previous generations possessed, and consequently, become dependent on others for things they used to provide for themselves. Power, social psychologist Richard Emerson (1981) reports, is a function of dependency. If we become dependent on someone for things we need, that person has power over us. Consequently, the more we turn responsibility for our lives over to others, the more dependent we become on them and the less influence we have over our own lives. In his excellent sociological treatise on chronic depression, Karp (1996) provides a vivid description of the condition of members of contemporary postindustrial societies:

> There can be little dispute that behavior in today's "postindustrial" society is dominated by "experts." Experts follow us through the life course, advising us on virtually every aspect of existence. They are there when we are born and accompany us each step along the way until we die. Among other things, we rely on experts to tell us how to maintain health, how to become educated, how to make love, how to raise children, and how to age correctly. (p. 173)

Freidson (1970) raises questions about personal autonomy and reliance on experts. He states:

> The relationship of the expert to modern society seems in fact to be one of the central problems of our time, for at its heart lie the issues of democracy and freedom and the degree to which [people] can shape the character of their own lives. The more decisions are made by experts, the less they can be made by laymen . . . I believe that expertise is more and more in danger of being used as a mask for privilege and power rather than, as it claims, as a mode of advancing the public interest. (p. 336-37)

While in many ways experts have blessed our lives, this blessing may come at the price of autonomy. Home schooling stands, in part, as a rejection of experts and represents a significant attempt of people to control their own lives. While there may be risks involved in this form of self reliance, one could easily argue that to blindly rely on the experts of the day comes with risks as well. Experts are at times incorrect in the wisdom they dispense and many people come to blindly accept their prescriptions and do not learn to think and act for themselves. Consequently, while some professional educators may be insulted by the existence of home schooling and its claim that parents who are not certified teachers can educate their own children, the philosophies and pedagogical methods that guide certified educators have not always worked, and many traditionally schooled students have not received a satisfactory education.

Other factors have influenced the emergence of home schooling as well. Sociologist Joel Best (1990) finds that while a concern for the safety and well-being of children has been embedded in American culture for many years, that concern intensified dramatically during the 1970s and 80s. During that time, the general public came to believe that children were threatened by a variety of malevolent forces from which they needed protection. Among other things, the political left feared the victimization of children at the hands of physical and sexual abusers while the political right feared the corrupting influences of an increasingly permissive and secular culture. Home schooling blossomed as this culture-wide fear about the vulnerability of children increased. I believe the timing of its emergence and growth in the 80s and 90s is, in part, a consequence of this widespread belief that children were in increasing peril and in need of protection from hostile world.

Dovetailing with this concern about threatened children was a growing national sentiment that public schooling was ineffective (Tyack 1991). It is noteworthy that while Americans have always suspected that public schools were not adequately educating children, that concern intensified during the 80s and 90s. A public document entitled *A Nation at Risk* decried the academic efficacy of public schooling arguing that "a rising tide of mediocrity" in public education was placing the nation at risk of becoming economically irrelevant (U. S. Department of Education 1983). The report became the genesis of a national political and media campaign emphasizing the troubles with public schooling. The image of schools as dangerous places where bullying, sexual harassment, and shootings were common also increased during this time culminating with the highly publicized school shootings that occurred in the 1990s. While it is debatable whether schools were increasingly dangerous and ineffective, perceptions are powerful things regardless of their veracity.

Returning to Mill's insight offered above involving the intersection of history and personal biography, the reasons parents give for choosing home schooling only matter in the context of a society that allows home schooling to exist in the first place. This is a society where discontent with traditional institutions is widespread to the point that alternatives to them are tolerated, where there is concern that children are at risk and where public schools are viewed with suspicion, mistrust and animosity by many. In other words, the existence of home schooling results from the success of people who have come to define traditional schooling and the prevailing culture as undesirable and have created an alternative that they perceive better meets their needs.

Conclusions

The home schooling experience is about relationships, socialization, and autonomy. In her controversial and insightful book, Harris (1998) argues that parenting has little impact on children and adolescents while peers have a substantial impact on them. She carefully reviews and critiques previous research studies that suggest parenting techniques matter, and she dismisses them as method-ologically flawed. Harris believes that as humans evolved, children spent much of their time with peers and little time with their parents. Furthermore, relying on twin studies and other research findings, she argues that genetic factors are more responsible for the human personality than parenting styles. Children are like their parents because they share their genes not because of the way they were raised.

Harris's work ignited a firestorm of debate. Critics raised concerns about the implications of her findings: Was she correct? If believed, would her findings prompt parents to conclude that their efforts are superfluous and to give up trying to influence their children for the good? Would errant parents use Harris as an excuse for their inattention and incompetence? While many would like to dismiss Harris, most people must acknowledge that there is at least some truth to her reasoning. That children have a genetic inheritance that makes them different from one another is immediately apparent, as Ridley (2003, 254) states, "to people who have more than one child." Each of my children, for example, has different emotional, cognitive, and behavioral orientations that cannot be explained by environment or birth order alone. They came into this world with their own unique temperaments, not as blank slates. We may have molded and shaped them some, but their basic temperaments remain intact. Harris is at least partly correct, but what does her work have to do with home schooling?

Like many others, we designed our home school to accommodate our son's unique characteristics. They shaped it as much if not more than it shaped them. A careful reading of Harris's work suggests that one of the reasons parenting style matters so little is that families are not true primary social groups. Sociologists define primary social groups as two or more people with strong, long-lasting bonds who interact with each other on a regular basis, have shared expectations for each others behaviors, and social boundaries stipulating who is and is not a member of a particular group. Most of our biological, emotional, and social needs are met by the primary groups to which we belong. Contemporary peer groups are arguably more primary in nature than many families. While Harris argues that human evolution separated children from their parents, I maintain that the structure of contemporary society has done so as well.

During the course of this study, I interacted with and interviewed a consider-able number of adolescents who were members of various youth groups I was involved with as an adult leader. After my interviews with them, my gut reaction was: *Of course Harris is correct. Parents and children are seldom together.* Most of the teens I worked with came from good homes and were fine young people who have gone on to accomplish much with their lives. Because of the structure of their lives, however, they interacted with their parents only in passing, during brief and hurried meals, or on their way to being dropped off at this activity or that. Most could not remember the last time they had a satisfying and meaningful conversation with their parents. From preschool to college, they were segregated from adults and they built their lives around their peers. As a sociologist, I do not look to evolution to explain the importance of peers and the unimportance of parents as shapers of children as Harris does; I look to the structure of contemporary society. How could parenting style matter very much when children and teens live lives apart from their parents?

Although it is not always successful, home schooling offers the opportunity for families to structure their lives in a way that allows for more interaction between parents and children than occurs in typical contemporary families. While I maintain that home schooled children retain their individuality, the structure of their lives places parents in a position to yield more influence over them and peers to yield less. While my sons are very different from each other and are going their own unique ways, we have relationships with them built of years of interaction that we would not have had had they attended traditional schools. Like many of their fellow home school students, they are bright and academically solid, but I'm not sure they would have been any less academically accomplished had they attended traditional schools. As a professor I work with many bright, personable, and responsible students who are products of traditional schools.

Home schooling did not alter our sons' innate temperaments very much, but it did reduce the degree of peer dependency they experienced, improved their relationships with us, and allowed our family greater autonomy over, and responsibility for, their personal lives. Most persistent home schooling families I know experienced the same outcomes. Ultimately, to them and to us, this is what home schooling was about.

Reference List

Adler, Patricia A. and Peter Adler. 1994. Social Reproduction and the Corporate Other: The Institutionalization of Afterschool Activities. *The Sociological Quarterly* 5:309-328.

Adler, Patricia A., Steven J. Kless, and Peter Adler. 1992. Socialization to Gender Roles: Popularity among Elementary School Boys and Girls. *Socioogy of Education* 65: 169- 87.

Anderson, Scott. 2007. Coming of Age at Band-I-Amir. National Geographic Adventure, May.

Babbie, Earl. 2005. *The Practice of Social Research, 3rd Edition.* New York: Wadsworth.

Bellah, Robert, Richard Madsen, William M. Sullivan, Ann Swidler, and Steven M. Tipton. 1991. *The Good Society.* New York: Vintage Books.

Bennett, Hal Z. 1972. *No More Public School.* New York: Random House.

Berger, Peter. 1963. *Invitation to Sociology: A Humanistic Perspective.* New York: Anchor.

Berliner, David C. and Bruce J. Biddle. 1995. *The Manufactured Crises: Myths, Fraud, and the Attack on America's Public Schools.* New York: Perseus Book.

Best, Joel. 1990. *Threatened Children: Rhetoric and Concern About Child-Victims.* Chicago: University of Chicago Press.

Blumer, Herbert. 1969. *Symbolic Interactionism: Perspective and Method.* Englewood Cliffs, New Jersey: Prentice Hall.

Brookover, Wilbur B. 1964. *A Sociology of Education.* New York: American Book Company.

Bynum, Jack E. and William E. Thompson. 1989. *Juvenile Delinquency: A Sociological Approach.* New York: Allyn and Bacon.

Chatham-Carpenter, April. 1994. Home versus Public Schoolers: Differing Social Opportunities. *Home School Researcher* 10: 15-24.

Colfax, David. and Micki. Colfax. *Homeschooling for Excellence*. New York: Time Warner Books.

Colomy, Paul. 2005. Three Sociological Perspectives. In *The Spirit of Sociology*, ed. Ron Matson, 32-42. New York: Allyn and Bacon.

Delahookie, Mona M. 1986. Home Educated Childrens Social/Emotional Adjustment and Academic Achievement: A Comparative Study. Unpublished doctoral dissertation. *Dissertation Abstracts International* 47: 475A.

Durkheim, Emile. 1961. On Mechanical and Organic Solidarity. In *Theories of Society: Foundations of Modern Sociological Thought*, eds. Talcott Parsons, Edward Shils, Kasper D. Naegele and Jesse R. Pitts, 208-12. New York: The Free Press.

Eckert, Penelope. 1989. *Jocks and Burnouts: Social Categories and Identity in the High School*. New York: Teachers College Press.

Elkin, Frederick and Gerald Handel. 1989. The Child and Society: The Process of Socialization, 5th edition. New York: McGraw Hill.

Elkind, David. 1995. School and Family in The Postmodern World. Phi Delta Kappan 77: 8-14.

———. 1998. *All Grown Up and No Place to Go*. New York: Addison Wesley.

Emerson, Richard. 1981. Social Exchange Theory. In *Social Psychology: Sociological Perspectives*, eds. Morris Rosenberg and Ralph H. Turner, 30-65. New York: Basic Books.

Foley, Douglas E. 1994. *Learning Capitalist Culture: Deep in the Heart of Tejas*. Philadelphia, Pennsylvania: University of Pennsylvania Press.

Friedson, Eliot. 1970. *Profession of Medicine: A Study of the Sociology of Applied Knowledge*. New York: Dodd, Mead and Company.

Gallagher, Winifred. 1994. How We Become What We Are. *The Atlantic Monthly*: 274: 38-64.

Gatto, John Taylor. 1992. *Dumbing Us Down: The Hidden Curriculum of Compulsory Schooling*. Philadelphia, Pennsylvania: New Society Publishers.

———. 1995. *The Exhausted School: Bending the Bars of Traditional Education*. Berkeley, California: Berkeley Hills.

Gecas, Viktor. 1982. The Self Concept. *Annual Review of Sociology* 8: 1-33.

Goffman, Erving. 1959. *The Presentation of Self in Everyday Life*. New York: Doubleday.

———. 1961. Asylums: Essays on the Social Situation of Mental Patients and Other Inmates. Chicago: Aldine Publishing Company.

Gottlieb, David, John Reeves and Warren. D. TenHouten. 1966. *The Emergence of Youth Societies: A Cross-Cultural Approach*. New York: The Free Press.

Gracey, Harry. 2001. Learning the Student Role: Kindergarten as Academic Boot Camp. In *Down to Earth Sociology: Introductory Readings, 11 ed.*, ed. James M. Henslin, 364-76. New York: The Free Press.

Guterson, David. 1992. *Family Matters: Why Homeschooling Makes Sense*. New York: Harcourt Brace.

———. 1998. No Longer a Fringe Movement. Newsweek, October 5.

Habermas, Jurgen. 1981. New Social Movements. *Telos*: 33-37.

Harris, Judith Rich. 1998. *The Nurture Assumption: Why Children Turn Out The Way They Do.* New York: The Free Press.

Hersch, Patricia. 1998. *A Tribe Apart: A Journey into the Heart of American Adolescence.* New York: Fawcett Columbine.

Holt, John. 1964. *Why Children Fail. Reading*, Massachusetts: Addison Wesley.

———. 1982. *Teach Your Own: A Hopeful Path for Education.* New York: Delta.

Illich, Ivan. 1971. *Deschooling Society.* New York: Harper Row.

Jackson, Philip W. 1968. *Life in Classrooms.* New York: Holt, Rinehart, Winston.

Karp, David A. 1996. *Speaking of Sadness: Depression, Disconnection, and the Meaning of Illness.* New York: Oxford University Press.

Kerr, Barbara A. 1985. *Smart Girls, Gifted Women.* Columbus Ohio: Ohio Psychology Publishing Company.

Knowles, J. Gary, Stacey. Marlow, and James A. Muchmore. 1992. From Pedagogy to Ideology: Origins and Phases of Home Education in the United States, 1970-1990. *American Journal of Education* 100: 195-235.

Kohn, Alfie. 1993. *Punished by Rewards.* New York: Houghton Mifflin.

Koontz, Dean. 2006. *The Husband.* New York: Bantam Books.

Kozol, Jonathan. 1992. *Savage Inequalities: Children in America's Schools.* New York: Harper Perenial.

Lines, Patricia. 1991. Home Instruction: The Size and Growth of the Movement. In *Home Schooling: Political, Historical, and Pedagogical Perspectives*, ed. Jane Van Galen and Mary Anne Pitman, 43-62. Norood, New Jersey: Ablex Publishing Company.

Llewellyn, Grace. 1991. *The Teenage Liberation Handbook.* Eugene, Oregon: Lowry House.

Lois, Jennifer. 2006. Role Strain, Emotional Management and Burnout: Homeschooling Mothers' Adjustment to the Teacher Role. Symbolic Interaction 29: 507-30.

Louv, Richard. 2005. *Last Child in the Woods: Saving Our Children from Nature-Deficit Disorder.* Chapel Hill, North Carolina: Algonquin Books.

Mayberry, Maralee, J. Gary Knowles, Brian Ray, and Stacey Marlow. 1995. *Home Schooling: Parents as Educators.* Thousand Oaks, California: Corwin Press.

McDowell, Susan A. 2004. *But What About Socialization? Answering the Perpetual Home Schooling Question, A Review of the Literature.* Nashville, Tennessee: Philodius Press.

Medlin, Richard G. 2000. Home Schooling and the Question of Socialization. *Peabody Journal of Education* 75: 107-23.

———. 1998. For Homeschooled Children, the Social Contacts are Diverse. *Homeschooling Today* 7(5):51-2.

Melucci, Alberto. 1989. *Nomads of the Present: Social Movements and Individual Needs in Contemporary Society.* Philadelphia, Pennsylvania: Temple University Press.

Merton, Don E. 2005. The Meaning of Meanness: Popularity, Competition, and Conflict Among Junior High School Girls. In *The Spirit of Sociology: A Reader*, ed. Ron Matson, 367-77. New York: Allyn and Bacon.

Mills, C. Wright. 2005. The Sociological Imagination. In *The Spirit of Sociology: A Reader*, ed. Ron Matson, 11-20. New York: Allyn and Bacon.

Milner, Murray, Jr. 2004. *Freaks, Geeks, and Cool Kids*. New York: Routledge.

Montgomery, Linda. 1989. The Effect of Home Schooling on the Leadership Skills of Home Schooled Students. *Home School Research* 5:1-10.

O'Brien, Jodi, ed. 2006. *The Production of Reality, 4th Ed*. Thousand Oaks, California: Pine Forge Press.

Orfield, Gary. 2001. Schools More Separate: Consequences of a Decade of Resegregation. Cambridge, Massachusetts: Civil Rights Project, Harvard University [online]. Retrieved April 9, 2007 from the World Wide Web: http://www.civilrightsproject.harvard.edu/research/deseg/separate_schools01.php

Olweus, Dan. 1993. Bullying at School: What We Know and What We Can Do. Maldon, Massachusetts: Blackwell Publishing.

Percy, Walker. 1985. Questions They Never Asked Me. In *Conversations with Walker Percy*, ed. Lewis A. Lawson and Victor A. Kramer, 178. Jackson, MS: University Press of Mississippi.

Price, Reynolds. 2001. *Feasting the Heart*. New York: Scribner Books.

Ray, Brian. 2004. *Home Educated and Now Adults*. Salem, Oregon; National Home Education Research Institute.

———. 1997. *Strengths of Their Own: Academic Achievement, Family Characteristics, and Longitudinal Traits*. Salem: Oregon: National Home Education Research Institute.

Ray, Brian and Jon Wartes. 1991. The Academic Achievement and Affective Development of Home-schooled Children. In *Home Schooling: Political, Historical, and Pedagogical Perspectives*, ed. Jane Van Galen and Mary Anne Pitman, 43-62. Norwood, New Jersey: Ablex Publishing Company.

Repp, Cheryl. 2005. Does Patriarchy Lead to Domestic Violence? Student Paper, Department of Sociology and Anthropology, Emporia State University.

Richman, Sheldon. 1995. *Separating School and State: How to Liberate America's Families*. Fairfax, Virginia: Future of Freedom Foundation.

Ridley, Matt. 2003. *Nature Via Nurture: Genes, Experience, and What Makes Us Human*. New York: HarperCollins.

Rosenberg, Morris. 1979. *Conceiving the Self*. New York: Basic Books.

Rosenfeld, Alvin and Nicole Wise. 2001. *The Overscheduled Child: Avoiding the Hyper-Parenting Trap*. St Martins Griffin.

Rudner, Lawrence M. 1999. Scholastic Achievement and Demographic Characteristics of Home School Students in 1998. *Educational Analysis Policy Archives* [Online]. Retreived April 6, 2007 from the World Wide Web: http://epaa.asu.edu/epaa/v7n8/

Schneider, Barbara, Mihaly Csikszentmihalyi, and Shaunti Knauth. 1995. Academic Challenge, Motivation, and Self Esteem: The Daily Experiences of Students in High School. In *Restructuring Schools: Promising Practices and Policies*, ed. Maureen T. Hallinan, 175-94. New York: Plenum.

Schneirov, Matthew and Jonathan David Geczik 1996. A Diagnosis for Our Times: Alternative Health's Submerged Networks and the Transformation of Identities. *Sociological Quarterly* 37: 627-44.

Schroll, Mark. 1988. Developments in Modern Physics and Their Implications for the Social and Behavioral Sciences. In *The Religion and Family Connection: Social Science Perspectives*, ed. Darwin L. Thomas, 303-23. Provo, Utah: Religious Studies Center, Brigham Young University.

Sebald, Hans. 1968. *Adolescence: A Sociological Analysis*. New York: Appleton-Century-Crofts.

Shyers, Larry E. 1992. Comparison of Social Adjustment Between Home and Traditionally Schooled Students. *Home School Research* 8: 1-8.

Stevens, Mitchell L. 2001. *Kingdom of Children: Culture and Controversy in the Homeschooling Movement*. Princeton, New Jersey: Princeton University Press.

Swann, Alexandra. 1989. *No Regrets: How Home Schooling Earned Me a Master's Degree at Age 16*. El Paso, TX: Cygnet Press.

Tallman, Irving, Ramona Marotz-Baden and Pablo Pindas. 1983. *Adolescent Socialization in Cross-Cultural Perspective: Planning For Social Change*. New York: Academic Press.

Thernstrom, Abigail and Stephan Thernstrom. 2003. No Excuses: Closing the Racial Gap in Learning. New York: Simon and Schuster.

Thomas, W. I. and Dorothy S. Thomas. 1928. *The Child in America*. New York: Knopf.

Thompson, William E and Joseph V. Hickey. 1996. *Society in Focus: The Essentials*. New York: Harper Collins.

Tuch, Steven A., Lee Sigelman, and Jason A. McDonald. 1999. Race Relations and American Youth, 1976-1995. *Public Opinion Quarterly* 63: 109-148.

Tyack, David. 1991. Public School Reform: Policy Talk and Institutional Practice. *American Journal of Education* 100: 1-19.

U. S. Department of Education. National Commission on Excellence in Education. 1983. *A Nation at Risk: An Imperative for Educational Reform* [online]. Retrieved April 9, 2007 from the World Wide Web: http://www.ed.gov/ubs/NatAtRisk/index.html.

Van Galen, Jane. 1991. Ideologues and Pedagogues: Parents Who Teach Their Children At Home. In *Home Schooling: Political, Historical, and Pedagogical Perspectives*, eds. Jane Van Galen and Mary Anne Pitman, 63-76. Norwood, New Jersey: Ablex Publishing Company.

Welner, Kariane Mari and Kevin G. Welner. 1999. Contextualizing Homeschool Data: A Response to Rudner. *Educational Policy Analysis Archives* [online]. Retrieved May 14, 2007 from the World Wide Web: http://epaa.asu.edu/ v7 n13/board/rud.html.

Wilder, Thornton. 1938. *Our Town: A Play in Three Acts*. New York: Coward McCann, Inc.

Wiseman, Rosalind. 2002. *Queen Bees and Wannabes: Helping Your Daughter Survive Cliques, Gossip, Boyfriends, and Other Realities of Adolescence*. New York: Three Rivers Press.

Index

ABOUT THE AUTHOR

Gary Wyatt earned his degrees from Utah State University in Logan, Utah, and Washington State University in Pullman, Washington. He has been a member of the faculty of the Department of Sociology and Anthropology at Emporia State University for nineteen years. He lives with his wife and sons in Emporia, Kansas.

www.ingramcontent.com/pod-product-compliance
Lightning Source LLC
Chambersburg PA
CBHW021823270326
41932CB00007B/319